# Bullish On Renewable Energy

*Fourteen Reasons that Clean Energy
Investors Can't Lose*

CRAIG SHIELDS

ISBN: 0692353410
ISBN: 9780692353417

Special Thanks to Gary Tulie

I can't begin to express my gratitude to my friend and colleague Gary Tulie for his enthusiastic support of this project, and, more to the point, for the enormous amount of content he contributed. His help enabled me to get this whole effort wrapped up far faster than I possibly could have if I had been forced to research every detail personally.

Gary is extremely bright, and was always eager to go in any direction I asked, which not only made the whole process totally enjoyable for me, but also served the reader quite well.

Bullish on Renewable Energy

Fourteen Reasons Why Clean Energy Investors Can't Lose

# Contents

# Part One:
## Clean Energy – A Success Story Being Written

We all know that our world is changing more quickly now than it has ever in the past. For instance, the pace at which information is being collected and published has accelerated to the point that half of the world's content is less than two years old, meaning that, astonishingly, we've generated as much content in the last 24 months as we had since the dawn of the species 200,000 years ago. And no one needs to be reminded that the rate at which technology, e.g., medical, communications, IT, etc., is changing our lives (we hope for the better) is many times what it was just a few decades ago.

It would be hard to list all the implications of this increase in "techno-velocity," though, fortunately for me, doing so isn't required, as only one of them is the subject of this book: the energy industry – examining the changes in the way energy is generated, transmitted, distributed, and ultimately used by businesses and consumers.

80% of the world's energy is derived from burning hydrocarbons—processes that are clearly unsustainable—but I contend that we're living in a time where fossil fuels will be replaced with clean energy in a very short period of time. Yes, I know I'm not the first person to lay a chip down on the rate of the demise of 20$^{th}$ Century energy in favor of something new. In fact, even Shell Oil says that by 2060, virtually all our energy will derive from the sun. When they say this, I presume they're referring to solar energy as a collection of several different varieties: photovoltaics, concentrated solar power, wind (energy from the pressure differentials caused by the sun's unequal heating of the Earth's surface), biomass (photochemically captured sunshine), hydrokinetics (energy from water that was moved around by the sun's energy), wave (energy from the wind, derived from the sun), etc.

Who knows what the folks at Shell really think about their life expectancy? Is there anyone foolish enough to think that they're laying their cards on the table? Regardless, I see this whole thing happening *far* before 2060, and the point of the next section of this book is simply to provide my reasons for this belief.

I'd love to say that the driver of all of this is our civilization's appreciation of the danger of things like oil and coal, and humankind's insistence that they be replaced with sources of energy that have far fewer negative consequences—and it's possible that this will prove to be at least partly true. Though the oil companies have spent hundreds of millions of dollars in the advertising and public relations campaigns to convince people that fossil fuels are the only legitimate form of inexpensive and reliable energy, and that renewables are an unworkable fad, it's clear that most people have begun to see through this. The Sierra Club's "Beyond Coal" message, perhaps the most effective of hundreds of similar campaigns, has already garnered the support of tens of millions of U.S. voters—and more join the ranks every week.

But the final nail in the coffin of fossil fuels will prove to be simple economics, rather than changing public sensibilities. Today, power purchase agreements for wind energy in certain parts of the U.S. are being signed at $0.02-$0.03/kilowatt-hour, a deal that is still extremely profitable for the developer of these wind projects. Note that this is far less than the cost of energy from coal.

Think of this for a minute. Under the right conditions (that are becoming more prevalent every day), we can generate clean energy far less expensively than we can generate electricity with coal-fired power plants. This will mean ridding ourselves of coal's incredible range of pollutants: not only the $CO_2$, but also the oxides of nitrogen and sulfur, as well as a range of heavy metals and radioactive isotopes; it's far and away the dirtiest and most lethal source of energy the planet has ever known.

## The Coming Hockey Stick

I've often compared what is happening in the energy industry with what happened in telephony a few years ago, i.e., the unpredicted boom in cell phone ownership/usage. In particular, we all remember how the great market research firms failed to make this prediction, forecasting some sort of linear expansion of cellular technology with a gradual and uninteresting effect on copper landlines. But a few years later we had five billion cell phones and a whole bunch of Brooks Brothers-clad MBAs with egg all over their faces.

I fully acknowledge that there are important differences in the energy and telephony markets, mainly regulation. But, as we'll see in the chapter on the power utilities, even this is unravelling quite rapidly.

## Why Investors Can't Miss

In this book, we'll explore how those who invest in clean energy over the coming years will find it very difficult to fail, given the great wealth of overwhelmingly positive circumstances that prevail today, and will only grow as time passes—both in number and in force.

The bulk of the book is a series of chapters, each centered on one of the major facts at play here. Again, at the risk of giving anything away, the overall driver is economics.

Yes, it would be good to have government support. It's possible that the United States will help the process along by stepping up and playing a leadership role as it's done many times in the past, though it sure is inert right now—a function of the unlovely confluence of money and politics.

A few strokes of a pen in the U.S. Congress could represent a big step in creating a level playing field for renewables, by making the primary tool for capital formation in oil and gas exploration, called master limited partnerships, or MLPs, legal for solar and wind as well. While they're at it, they could get rid of the enormous subsidies we provide to the oil companies—a 90-year-old industry, the most profitable one in the history of civilization. Am I counting on it? Of course not.

Perhaps the International Panel on Climate Change will miraculously bring the nations of the world into harmony and understanding. I interviewed IPCC's chairman, Dr. Rajendra Pachauri, for my most recent book, and it's clear that he's an honest, hardworking person trying his heart out to make progress here, but he sure does seem to be hitting a brick wall.

Or we can hope that the impetus will come from the world's people themselves, somehow beginning to act as brothers and sisters, rising together as one to manifest a new-found respect for Mother Earth.

In truth, there are many possible events that could accelerate the demise of fossil fuels—but none is required to phase them out in favor of renewables, which can (and probably will) be *driven purely by market economics*. Thus the main point of the book: the move to clean energy will happen far more rapidly than most people imagine, based on the sheer power of financial pressures exerting themselves on the energy market.

I'm reminded of the Econ 101 class I took freshman year, where our professor lovingly referred to economics as the "mother discipline," meaning, of course, that this is the arena in which all practical concerns are resolved. "In what field do you plan to major, Mr. Shields?" he called on me at random the first week of class, startling me slightly. "Ah, physics, sir," I responded. "Splendid, Mr. Shields. I'm sure that, at some point in your life, you'll contribute some excellent new ideas to that fascinating subject. But do you know what will determine whether those ideas ever see the light of day in the real world, outside your office walls?" I simply nodded and smiled. He had made his point without the need for either of us to verbalize the answer to his question.

## The Tipping Point

Malcolm Gladwell popularized the phrase "tipping point" with his 2007 book. Another way of explaining the main of the book you're about to read is that it provides a list of the reasons I believe that renewable energy has arrived at precisely that moment, i.e., the flashpoint at which the world of energy transforms itself. We've been rolling the ball uphill until now, but we've reached the top, and the ball will now be on its way down the other side—in one heck of a hurry.

Now, let's turn our attention to the matter at hand: a journey through the main concepts that explain why that the force of economics alone is sufficient to cause the demise of the fossil fuel industry in a surprisingly short period of time.

# Part Two:

## Fourteen Reasons Why Clean Energy Will Successfully Replace Fossil Fuels in the Very Near Future

# Chapter One—
# Energy Efficiency: The Much Ballyhooed "Low-Hanging Fruit"

Everybody loves efficiency, as it's by far the easiest and least expensive place to turn to reduce the eco-footprint of energy. But we need to ask why the subject of efficiency is relevant to the question at hand. I.e., how will efficiency help renewable energy skyrocket to prominence, replacing fossil fuels? The answer is the size of the overall energy "pie," and the capacity of renewable energy to scale in order to address that effectively.

For example, there are many extremely intelligent and studious people who advocate for advanced nuclear energy as the low-carbon energy solution for the 21st Century. As readers will see in the next chapter, they're running headlong into people who believe that all nuclear is dangerous, and hold onto this belief with such rabid tenacity that they are unwilling to consider that a next-gen nuclear technology could be safe and cost-effective. In any case, advocates of nuclear argue that renewable energy cannot be developed in sufficient volume in time to avert the climate crisis because of the enormity of energy consumption/load and its expected growth over the coming few decades. The strength of their case is directly related to the overall size of that load. A smaller pie, which can and will be served at least in part by efficiency and conservation solutions, means a weaker argument for nuclear—and for fossil fuels as well.

Let's provide a short survey of some of today's most important themes in efficiency, many of which technologies depend on capturing and recycling heat.

## Combined Heat & Power (CHP) and Tri-generation

Traditional fossil-fueled power stations burn fuel to create mechanical power which is then converted into electricity. Due to thermodynamic limitations imposed by the ideal Carnot cycle, combined with losses in the conversion of mechanical power to electricity, power stations are only able to recover around 40% to 55% of the energy in the fuel in the form of electricity. Having captured this power, the remaining energy in the fuel is typically discharged through a cooling tower, serving no useful purpose.

In CHP mode, rather than discharge this heat to the air or to water, the heat is recovered, so allowing up to around 80% of the chemical energy in the fuel to serve a useful purpose.

Possibly the widest deployment of CHP is in Denmark, where for several decades, there has been a prohibition on discharging heat from thermal power stations through cooling towers. Instead, Denmark's power stations are water-cooled, and the hot water that is generated supplies heat to the country's many district heating networks. As a result, over 60% of Denmark's homes are heated and have their hot water largely provided by waste heat from the country's thermal power stations.

In addition to district heating, CHP is also useful for industrial customers with simultaneous high demand for electricity and heat, such as food factories. For example, consider a large food-processing factory which may choose to install a CHP engine. Electricity is provided by the mechanical power of the engine, high temperature "dry" steam for cooking is generated by heat recovered from the exhaust, and sanitary hot water from the radiator.

Taking the above process one step further, it is possible to take some of the heat and use it to drive an adsorption cooling system to chill the cooked food prior to packing and freezing. This process is called "tri-generation," and in some cases achieves up to 90% utilisation of the chemical energy in the fuel.

## Power Generation from Industrial Waste Heat

Some industrial processes use a great deal of high temperature heat, e.g., the manufacture of cement and steel.

Cement and steel are used in huge quantities, involve very high temperature processes in their manufacture, and result in the discharge of huge amounts of heat from the back end of the process at temperatures typically between 200C and 400C.

Global production of cement is forecast to reach 4.8 billion tons per annum by 2017 – with a manufacturing process which typically involves heating raw materials to >1450C. Steel production meanwhile was 1.65 billion tons in 2012 with a broadly similar process temperature- so implying a huge potential to recover heat for other industrial processes and electricity generation.

According to the "Industrial Efficiency Technology Database – Waste Heat Recovery for Power Generation," Japan has 33 co-generation plants of this nature which together generate 200 MW of power using heat which would otherwise be wasted.

## Evaporative Cooling Rather than Air Conditioning

In regions with high temperatures and relatively low humidity, it is possible to cool buildings to comfortable temperatures by evaporative cooling; such systems are particularly attractive in regions where there is little or no requirement for winter heating.

Whereas an air conditioning unit might at best achieve a coefficient of performance (COP-- the ratio of electricity in to heating or cooling out) of 4 or 5, evaporative cooling can be achieved using 90% less electricity. An immersion heater has at best a COP of 1 i.e., 1 kW of electricity in to 1 kW of heat out. An air conditioning unit might achieve 4 or 5 kW of heating or cooling by using 1 kW of electricity, and an evaporative cooling unit or misting fan in very hot dry conditions, up to 40 kW of cooling for 1 kW of electricity in.

It is possible to use sea water for evaporative cooling, and processes are available by which sea water is first evaporated by sun and wind in the side wall of a greenhouse, then the resulting moisture is recaptured within the greenhouse as fresh water by passing it over a heat exchanger containing the incoming cold sea water. Such greenhouses can produce large crops in hot coastal desert areas while simultaneously producing more water than is required for their irrigation—up to 100,000 liters per day per 2.4 acres of greenhouse.

## Drain Water Heat Recovery

In a few situations, such as commercial laundries, hot water is used almost continuously. Where this is the case, it is possible to preheat the cold feed to the water heater by use of a heat exchanger so that less additional heat is required to achieve the desired temperature. Typically around 60% reduction in hot water energy demand can be achieved using this technique.

## Mechanical Heat Recovery Ventilation

In order to minimize heating load, buildings are increasingly well insulated and sealed. Whilst this is good for keeping heat in the building, if there is too little ventilation, air quality suffers and humidity can rise to levels which are not healthy for the building and its occupants. To overcome this difficulty while retaining heat within the building, mechanical heat recovery ventilation can be employed. By passing the exiting warm moist air through a heat exchanger, almost 90% of the heat in the expired air can be recovered and transferred to the incoming ventilation air, cutting heat losses to levels not achievable with natural ventilation. Where air conditioning is in use, this is advantageous in both summer and winter; in summer, the cooling effect of the air conditioning unit is retained while in winter, heat is not as easily lost.

Mechanical heat recovery ventilation is an essential part of achieving the Passivehaus standard for building energy efficiency.

## A Few Terrific Energy Efficiency Solutions

The reason that efficiency is the so-called "low-hanging fruit" in the quest to reduce the environment damage associated with providing energy to the world is that the ROI associated with efficiency makes it super-attractive. Since approximately 40% of our energy is consumed in our buildings, principally lighting and HVAC, the market for solutions in this arena—sustainable building products and related services—is in the process of a huge expansion, including many dozens of cutting-edge concepts.

Efficiency will be important in keeping the world energy growth curve under control over the coming 40 years, as the world population tops nine billion, and a large percentage of these people use more energy per capita than ever before in history. We need to keep in mind, however, that even with these efficiency solutions, the global demand for energy will double by 2050. Thus, there need to be many other factors, based purely on market economics, that militate in the direction of clean energy. Fortunately, there are.

# Chapter Two—
# The Development of Advanced Nuclear Reactors Will Be a Big Help

Most proponents of clean energy exclude nuclear from the list of options, because of the dangers associated with operating the solid fuel light water reactors that became available 50 – 60 years ago, and the challenges of dealing with the waste they create. However, we need to keep in mind that it's conceivable that nuclear can be made inexpensive and safe, and, if that's the case, it is irresponsible for advocates of clean energy to try to block progress in this direction.

If the possibility of safe nuclear is to be realized, in will most likely happen through molten salt reactors (MSRs), discussed at a high level below. In particular, we'll see how the decay of thorium (T232/U233) follows a completely different path than U235 and

U238, and we'll learn that thorium is a fairly abundant element, which comes to us as a byproduct of our current mining efforts. Indeed, its use in nuclear reactors has the potential to be safe in every sense of the word.

At the dawn of the nuclear age, the U.S. government was confronted with a choice between several different reactions, and chose the solid fuel light water reactor because it essentially killed two birds with one stone; it would simultaneously develop nuclear energy to power our country and form the basis of modern weaponry that we thought was such a great idea at the time.

We can now see (even if we somehow couldn't before) that this was a regrettable decision. Now we have a subject that has proven operationally dangerous, results in radioactive waste whose disposal is extremely problematic, and a set of processes that enable some of the world's most sinister forces to develop nuclear weapons. Having said that, MSRs hold the promise of being safe (low pressure), efficient (high temperature), non-threatening (very low weapons potential), and harmless to posterity (very little nuclear waste).

Here's more on the subject, an excerpt from Los Angeles writer Mike Conley's forthcoming book about MSRs and thorium, titled *"Power to the Planet."* Nuclear physicists may object to its simplicity, but I believe most readers will appreciate it.

## Forget everything you know about nuclear energy.

*The Molten Salt Reactor is a completely different kind of nuclear energy system, as different as an electric motor from a gasoline engine. It can't melt down, it can't blow up, and it won't spread contaminants, even if it's damaged or destroyed. It makes a small amount of short-term waste, and it can even use the nuclear waste from other reactors as a secondary fuel.*

**The MSR uses liquid fuel**—*nuclear material dissolved in molten (melted) fluoride salt. The major contaminants that spoil solid fuel rods are gases, which become trapped in solid fuel rods. But these gases bubble right out of liquid fuel, making the reactor much more efficient while producing much less waste.*

**The MSR can't have a meltdown,** *even if someone tried to make it happen. The reason is simple: How do you melt a liquid?*

**The MSR doesn't need external cooling.** *Liquid fuel acts as its own coolant by flowing out of the core, through the power generating system, and back again.*

**An MSR can be installed anywhere on earth**, *even an underground vault. A tsunami or tornado would roll right over it, like a truck over a manhole cover.*

**The MSR always operates at ambient pressure,** *with no volatile chemical reactions that could forcefully eject any harmful material.*

**If disaster strikes and the fuel leaks out**, *the spill cools to an inert lump of rock, chemically locking the material inside. Radioactive particles won't spread downwind or downstream, and the material can be recovered and used again.*

**A molten salt spill** *would be measured in square meters, not square kilometers.*

**An MSR generates twice the heat of a Light Water Reactor,** *and more heat equals more power. It can deliver direct 750°C heat for industrial processes, such as smelting and refining; the production of hydrogen; the production of ammonia for fertilizer and fuel; the clean conversion of* *coal, tar, and shale into liquid fuels; and perhaps most importantly, the desalination of seawater, wherever it's needed.*

**The MSR is highly resistant to proliferation.** *Repurposing the reactor for weapons production would be exceptionally difficult, and not worth the trouble. Much better proliferation options exist, with long and reliable track records.*

**The MSR is the best choice for producing nuclear energy,** *and the worst choice for producing nuclear weapons.*

**MSRs can utilize any nuclear fuel, even nuclear waste, but their ultimate fuel is thorium.** *Slightly radioactive thorium becomes highly radioactive uranium-233 inside the MSR, where nearly 99% of it is consumed. MSRs will significantly reduce the fabrication, transport, and disposal of dangerous nuclear material.*

**Thorium fuel produces a fraction of the long-term "waste" made in traditional uranium reactors.** *That's because thorium works at the low end of the nuclear fuel cycle by converting to Uranium-233, which has a 92% rate of fission. The final 8% converts to Uranium-235, which has an 85% rate of fission. That's a combined fission rate of 98.8%.*

**Thorium is more common than tin,** *and is found all over the world. There is no "Middle East of Thorium". The material is easily separated from other ores with low-tech, low-waste processes; it's good to go, right out of the ground. And it's so mildly radioactive that you could sleep on a slab of solid thorium your entire life, and the worst thing that could happen would be if you fell out of bed.*

**America has already mined enough thorium to power the country for 400 years.** *It's found in the waste piles of our abandoned Rare Earth Element mines. We mistakenly closed our REE mines in an overabundance of misguided caution, because thorium was in the waste stream.*

*Rare Earth and thorium are always found together. If thorium was used as fuel instead of being treated like a radioactive hazard, we could use it to power the entire country, and revive our domestic Rare Earth industry at the same time. This would bring our high-tech industries back home, and supply 40% of global Rare Earth requirements as well.*

*The "waste stream" of the wind turbine industry could power the planet. Neodymium is used for the magnets in windmill generators. The wind industry produces a tiny fraction of global power, and throws away the fuel needed to power the entire planet. (The good news is, we can dig it out of the trash.)*

*Rare Earth is a vital ingredient in our high-tech world, used in everything from earbuds to cell phones to guided missiles. But now that we've closed our mines, China controls 95% of the market, forcing many of our high-tech industries to move there to ensure access to the material. America's defense industry has become completely dependent on Rare Earth from China.*

*Liquid fuel changes everything. Since the fuel circulates in and out of the reactor, it can be continuously cleaned of the contaminants that spoil solid fuel rods, even while the MSR is operating at full power. This unique feature enables MSRs to consume fuel so thoroughly that they can even use the spent fuel from Light Water Reactors.*

*Nuclear waste is wasted fuel. MSRs will significantly reduce our existing stockpile of nuclear waste, including the material from dismantled nuclear weapons. Using long-term waste as fuel will break it down into short-term waste, shortening its toxic life from 10,000 years to 500 years.*

*The people who love to hate nuclear waste should be clamoring for MSRs. Because there are only two things you can do with nuclear waste—consume it as fuel, or bury it for 1,000 centuries. Mother Nature gives us no other choice.*

*An MSR can power a city on two teaspoons of thorium an hour. A 1-gigawatt MSR, large enough to power a metropolis of one million people, will run on one tonne (1,000 kgs) of thorium per year, for a fuel cost of about $300,000.*

*Most of the waste (83%) will mellow out in 1-10 years. The remainder will be the size of two basketballs, becoming low-level waste in about 500 years.*

*An MSR can be built as cheaply as a coal plant. In fact, they're actually much cheaper, because they would save the thousands of people each year that coal pollution would otherwise sicken and kill.*

*Coal kills 13,000 Americans a year. In China, the yearly death toll is over 100,000. Aside from all the pain and suffering and the loss of productivity, health care and environmental damage are just two of the "externalized" costs that society spends for dirty power, year after year.*

*There hasn't been a single death in America from commercial nuclear power. And we've been using it for over 50 years.*

## *A Molten Salt Reactor:*

- *Can't blow up.*
- *Can't melt down. Ever.*
- *The fuel is cheap and plentiful.*
- *It can use nuclear waste for fuel.*
- *It's as cheap to build as a coal plant.*
- *It's highly resistant to weapons proliferation.*
- *It can be re-fueled while it's running at full power.*

- *It generates much less waste than a regular reactor.*
- *The waste it does make is benign in a fraction of the time.*
- *It doesn't need water cooling, and can be installed anywhere.*
- *It's a proven technology, with 22,000 hours of trouble-free operation.*

*What are we waiting for?*

## *The MSR is an American invention*

*A national rollout of Molten Salt Reactors will create thousands of good jobs in every region of America, and launch a new paradigm of safe, cheap, and abundant carbon-free domestic energy.*

*A national thorium infrastructure was visualized by the Kennedy administration as far back as 1962. Ten years later, the Nixon Administration defunded the program, even though the test reactor ran without a hitch for nearly five years.*

*While a lot of useful R&D has been done since then, the MSR is still on the drawing board. But with sufficient funding (probably less than $5 billion), a working model is a realiztic five-year goal, and another five years for a national rollout is entirely feasible.*

## *This isn't rocket science*

*It's not high school chemisty, either, but going to the moon was a whole lot harder. And before that, in the dark days of WW II, we geared up overnight to build thousands of ships, tanks and bombers (not to mention the Manhattan Project) and we did it without computers or cell phones. So there's no reason to think we can't do it again, because when you get right down to it, the MSR is just a kettle of molten salt with high-temperature, low-pressure plumbing. In fact, they used to call it the 3P Reactor—it's essentially a pot, a pipe, and a pump.*

## *Made in China?*

*In the fall of 2010, a Chinese delegation toured Oak Ridge National Labs. Under a collaboration agreement between the Department of Energy and the Chinese Academy of Science, several subsequent meetings were held in which we shared our molten salt technology with them.*

*All geo-politics and competition aside, this sounds hopeful for the future of MSR and the expansion of carbon-free energy for the planet. But if we drop the ball again, the Chinese won't. And they promised to patent every advance they make.*

## *Bringing it all back home*

*Molten salt technology has languished on our drawing boards for decades, but now it's on China's drawing boards as well. And they mean business. So if we don't follow through this time, we will soon be buying our own invention from them.*

## *This is our Sputnik Moment.*

Let me close this chapter with a comment on the author's assertions concerning the time (five years) and the costs ($5 billion) required for the R&D. I recall a three-way call I had assembled in which I had on the phone both an inventor of a new hydrokinetic device and the director of technology at Black and Veatch, one of the world's largest engineering firms. Here's a snippet of the conversation:

*Inventor*:  And the best part is that this is going to be super-cheap to build.

*Director of Technology*:  We have a saying around here: "It's *always* cheap......until you build it."

But are we doomed if advanced nuclear doesn't fulfill the promises made here?  Not by a long shot.

# Chapter Three—
# Cheap Wind

In many parts of the world, energy from wind is extremely inexpensive. For example, PPAs (power-purchase agreements) written today in the U.S. are being signed at $0.02-$0.03/kilowatt-hour in the "plains" states, i.e., the central U.S., where capacity factors are high (in many cases over 50%); this is simply a result of supply and demand, i.e., the supply is huge and the demand is limited until we increase our capacity to ship power over longer distances.

Now, I fully expect readers to call this low figure into question, as it's not well documented—in part because the PPAs are confidential, and also since estimates of the levelized cost of energy (LCOE) from wind are much higher than this. But keep in mind that the LCOE numbers are based on the construction costs that developers report (perhaps $2.10 per watt), and those developers don't want their customers to know how much profit they're making, lest the negotiations become much tougher. The wind energy pundits I've interviewed tell me that the true installed cost of a wind turbine today is *far* under $2.10 per watt.

Even with a PPA at $0.02, when combined with a production tax credit of another $0.02, wind developers do just fine—even though these wind-rich areas, regrettably, have relatively low populations. Those who can somehow ship their power to the surrounding states where the rates are higher, e.g., Alabama, do even better.

Thus we see that energy from wind can be far cheaper than energy from coal (not that we're thinking about building new coal plants in the U.S.). Even with storage (perhaps via compressed air) and transmission, these pundits predict that the cost of energy from wind as baseload will be about $0.06 in a few short years.

## Numerous Factors Convene To Reduce the Cost of Wind Power

The cost of wind power is declining steadily, due to a combination of factors involving technical innovation in turbine design, more efficient manufacturing systems (we're been through a significant learning curve), better wind prospecting techniques, and reductions in the cost of associated systems such as power electronics and transmission technologies.

Within the wind industry, there are two main segments.

**Onshore Wind**. As we stated above, in some areas the technology can compete directly against all other technologies even without taking into account the environmental costs of pollution from the sources it's replacing.

The optimum size for a turbine is now generally in the range of 1.5 MW to 3 MW which varies slightly from market to market.

The object of the game is to achieve the lowest levelized cost of electricity (LCOE). To capture more power with a wind turbine, you can either make it taller, or increase the swept area of the blades. There is a complex balance between the cost of using longer blades / taller towers, the amount of extra power that can be captured, and engineering considerations such as wear and tear, and survival through extreme wind events.

Longer blades tend to increase materials' weight proportional to the cube of the length, while wind capture rises with the square. Accordingly, there comes a point where for a given blade design, a longer blade becomes too costly or too heavy to be cost effective.

At this time, turbines larger than 3 MW tend to increase rather than reduce the cost of wind power for land-based turbines. Turbines form a large proportion of the cost of an installed wind farm, and O&M (operations and maintenance) costs are lower than offshore, so there is nothing to be gained by reducing the number of turbines for a given wind farm rating beyond a certain point, especially where the cost per kilowatt-hour from the turbine increases.

**Offshore Wind.** Here, technologies are less mature and costs are higher, but they are declining faster due to being at an earlier stage in the learning curve.

The optimum size here appears to be over 6 MW; MHI Vestas has commercialized an 8 MW turbine with a 164 meter sweep. Few people realize how big this is; the swept area of this turbine is equal to three soccer fields.

Future turbines are expected to get even larger as foundations, cable connections, and O&M all form a far larger component of levelized cost of electricity than onshore; larger turbines mean fewer foundations, fewer cable connections, and fewer units to maintain.

This being the case, a larger turbine, even if its cost per kW is higher, can be cost-effective if the extra turbine costs are offset by greater savings elsewhere in the overall wind farm package. Foundations, cabling, and O&M only increase slightly with larger offshore turbine size, so the industry demands ever larger turbines. Thus, higher towers, larger generators and longer blades become an attractive means to lower levelized cost of electricity.

Prototype wind turbines rated at 10 MW are at an advanced stage of design, and likely to begin deployment shortly, while even larger turbines up to 20 MW are at the early research concept stage. It remains to be seen how big offshore turbines will eventually get but it is a fair assumption that those over 10 MW will eventually become the norm for this market segment.

Within the offshore wind industry, there is an emerging subsection of floating wind turbines. With fixed offshore wind turbines, there is a limit to viable water depth which limits suitable sites to areas with water depth up to around 30 meters. Floating designs allow deeper waters to be exploited, greatly increasing the number of potential sites for offshore wind power, and allowing the turbines to be placed further out to sea in areas with better wind resources.

With further R&D and volume production, it is likely that floating wind farms can match, or possibly even better the costs of fixed offshore wind power.

OK, now let's look at wind energy more generally, and ask ourselves how, exactly, costs are lowering:

- Wind farms are tending to get larger, bringing economies of scale, and the costs of building high towers is falling, especially in these large wind farms.

- Manufacturers are getting smarter as to how they manufacture turbine blades; the blades are becoming more precisely manufactured, with automated fiber lay-up and vacuum forming becoming the norm. Even with the same materials, such blades have more precisely tailored stiffness, greater strength, and lighter weight, allowing longer blades to be made without becoming too heavy. These techniques also reduce the costs of high volume blade construction.

- Some materials such as carbon fiber are dropping in cost as volumes manufactured for other industries increase, allowing more carbon fiber to be cost-effectively integrated into a turbine blade. Aerodynamic refinements are also being developed to allow pitch optimization at different points along the blade, using multiple ailerons; this increases yield while reducing blade loading in gusty conditions. It also helps to reduce blade weight and allows longer blades for a given nominal turbine rating.

- The above factors taken together mean that the optimum size of turbines is increasing as the cost-effective manufacture of high towers and longer blades is developed, while at the same time, capacity factors are increasing even where wind farms are installed in lower wind-speed areas.

- Advancements in power electronics (major components of wind turbines and wind farms) steadily reduce inverter costs and improve efficiency and power density, especially with the newer silicon carbide and gallium nitride semiconductors. In turn, higher power density reduces the weight of equipment, lowering costs elsewhere in the chain of production, such as transportation and crane use. Lower costs and better power electronics are also allowing higher voltage transmission; the new ABB ultra-high voltage DC system—operating at 1100 kV - which enables a set of power lines to transmit up to 10

GW of power over a distance of up to 3000 km. This allows for the possibility of installing ultra large wind farms in very remote areas with superb wind resource and transmitting large amounts of power to populated areas.

For example, Southern Morocco and Mauritania have huge areas where mean wind speeds at hub height are close to 10 m/s, where there are never hurricanes, and where the wind almost never stops. Such sites come very near to offering baseload electricity due to their exceptional wind resource, but until recently, they have been too remote to justify the infrastructure required to take power to market in Europe and Sub-Saharan Africa. Developments such as ultra-high voltage DC (UHVDC) are changing the economics of such potential projects and allowing them to be considered as part of a cost effective program to reduce greenhouse gases.

• Forward-looking LIDAR (a laser analogue of radar) is being developed. By incorporating LIDAR into wind turbines, it is possible to monitor incoming wind in precise three-dimensional detail including up-drafts and turbulence. This allows blade pitch and other control mechanisms to be adjusted according to predicted gusts rather than waiting for the gust to strike. In turbulent conditions, this can allow higher power yields while protecting the turbines from some of the loadings they would otherwise face - reducing O&M costs, and potentially allowing longer turbine blades to be used in a given wind regime.

• Wind farm modelling is becoming far more sophisticated, as is understanding of things like "wake effect," i.e., wind shadow, where one row of turbines interferes with some of the wind received by the row behind. This enables better wind farm layout and design, and improves the manner in which the turbines are managed to be better optimized, so that some increase in wind farm yield can be achieved even with the same number of the same turbines.

- Wind farm output forecasting is improving so that wind farms selling power onto forward markets, i.e., 4 to 24 hours ahead, face fewer costs buying and selling on the immediate spot market to cover under- or over-estimation of sold power output.

- For very large future turbines, 10 MW and larger, it is likely that super-conducting magnets cooled by liquid nitrogen will be incorporated within generators; this will greatly reduce the weight and size of such generators, and allow them to be more easily and cost effectively lifted to the turbine nacelle – possibly 150 meters or more above the sea. Once such technology is refined, it is likely to reduce the cost of very large turbines quite significantly.

- Operation and maintenance costs are steadily falling. Manufacturers are constantly learning how to make turbines more reliable, and how to optimize scheduled maintenance to reduce breakdowns. As a result, turbines are now available to generate power for more hours a year than ever before, and the cost of maintenance per MWh generated has never been lower. After the initial capital cost of the wind farm, O&M costs are the largest component of the cost of wind generated electricity.

- The world of financing for wind is improving as well; wind power is now sufficiently mature, and yields are sufficiently predictable to give a high level of confidence of returns, thus reducing the risk component of financing cost.

Adding electrical transmission capacity is not as expensive as most people believe, though this is something of a moot point, since, certainly in the U.S., the build-out of our grid needs to happen regardless of the migration to renewable energy. Building high-voltage AC transmission is extremely inexpensive, as it can be done directly over our existing medium-voltage lines; this makes the subject less noncontroversial as well, as it requires no new footprint/right-of-way.

# Chapter Four—
## Cheap Solar

Solar PV is becoming inexpensive too. Utility scale deals for solar photovoltaics are being signed now at about $0.05/kwh. Further, there is no need to couple solar energy with storage, as it corresponds fairly nicely to peak loads.

Recently, I had the opportunity to speak with my colleague Shawn Kravetz who runs Esplanade Capital, a major hedge fund in solar PV. As I recalled from a webinar I conducted with Shawn a few years ago, he's bullish on solar for a whole host of reasons. Here's an updated list of those reasons, based on what he told me quite recently:

- Solar is still very small, and there is so much room to grow; we've just started to scratch the surface, in this country, for example. The U.S. will grow 50% this year to 6.5 gigawatts, but that's less than Germany installed in 2010. Or 2011. Or 2012. We can argue that Germany over-invested, and the U.S. and other countries will have learned from that experience, but the bottom line is that solar is still very small with virtually unlimited room to grow. Solar represented 9% in Italy last month, but in most countries that matter, it's still under 1%. It could quadruple and still be tiny.

- Over the past decade, there has been a massive over-investment, largely through subsidies. Germany, Spain, and China overbuilt capacity. All these phenomena have led to lower costs, and thus lower prices for solar today. If not for all that, solar prices would be higher, and solar would be less competitive. The massive over-investment over the past decade or so has lowered the cost. Related to that, lower prices has continued to open up more and more markets around the world. This is especially true where there are still subsidies, which, by the way, are disappearing, either on a planned or unplanned schedule. This requires that solar be competitive—both the panels and the installation thereof, given that the subsidies are declining.

- Volumes continue to ramp, because of lower prices and better financing options, which I'll get back to in a moment. When we started investing in solar 11 years ago, there was 1 gigawatt installed. Now it's over 45 gigawatts. That's 45X growth in 11 years.... pretty dramatic. This year it's growing somewhere between the high teens to about 25% per year in annual installations.

- Markets have become more stable. For many years, Europe represented two-thirds of all solar installation. That's no longer the case; Europe crashed. But it's starting to rebound off a much more sustainable base. The U.S. is a very stable market for at least the next year or so. We're finally big enough here that really matters. China will be the biggest market in the world this year and next, and, though I'm reluctant to call anything in China "stable," it's fairly clear that they'll grow nicely at least this year and next, and will shoulder a significant amount of solar demand. Japan is unpredicatable, but there are enough markets of size and scale that just the overall aggregate demand is less vulnerable to single events, like Germany elections or what might be happening in Spain. That's how you grow a long term enduring industry. In the medium term, both China and India are targeting 100 GW of installed solar capacity – China is projected to possibly reach 100 GW as early as 2018, while India is aiming for 100 GW by 2022.

- There are some terrific companies. These are not companies that are dependent on the next big thing out of Silicon Valley, and they're not wholly dependent on largesse of a certain country; these are legitimate companies that have been slugging it for out a decade now, in many cases; they're as big as they've ever been, and they know how to run their businesses. Companies that have endured catastrophic downturns, and now know how to thrive. Trina, Yingli, Canadian Solar, Jinko, and Western companies like First Solar, Sun Power, and SunEdision; they're surviving. They're doing what they need to in order to compete, having weathered some pretty horrendous storms over the past several years.

- Let's talk about "financial engineering," which is usually a phrase that sounds derogatory, but I don't mean it that way. It comes in two parts. The first is the finance that allows people to "go solar" without doing things they can't do. Most people can't write a check for a $30,000 system. They can't be bothered to go through all the paperwork and understand how the tax credits and the renewable energy credits work. They do, however, know how to pay their electricity bills, and if they can save money and do something they want to do, that becomes interesting. And companies like Solar City in this country are making that happen; they're talking about installing a gigawatt...next year. That's one company, one market (the U.S.), and even one segment of that market (residential and small commercial). That is transformational.

The other side is the differentiation in what solar companies are offering, and that is the rise of the "yieldco" (which refers to large solar companies keeping projects on their balance sheets and paying out relatively attractive yields to investors). I'm skeptical about all the excitement, but it's clear that they are here to stay, and they have billions of dollars of market capitalization, and they provide an important function, in that they're kind of like garbage disposals for solar projects. The demand to fill those pipelines with solar projects that can throw off cash flows and dividends for their investors has never been greater. We see tremendous demand for project development and project developers to fill those pipelines; thus we will see this robust yieldco market continue to roll along. The point here is that this represents another huge source of projects, and those projects need panels.

- Last but not least, storage is coming. We think there is enough incentive, IP, etc., that there will be meaningful improvement in technology that will provide yet another uptick to solar. It's the icing on the cake.

Now, let's discuss a few other elements of the solar energy scene, and how it's improving steadily.

## The Costs of Solar Thermal Are Coming Down Too

The phrase "solar thermal" has different meanings.

## Solar Water Heating

The simplest common form of solar thermal is solar water heating – which already exists at very high penetration levels in many countries.

In Cyprus, a large majority of households as well as many hotels and most vacation apartments have solar water heaters, which offer the least-cost way of heating water for these users. Israel and parts of Spain now require solar water heating on all new houses as part of their building regulations. If designed into a new house, and installed when scaffold and tradespeople are already in place, costs are substantially lower than for a retrofit, and returns on investment are now favorable in many markets.

China and India have several million solar water heaters each, and large numbers of new ones are installed every year. Solar water heating is highly efficient and is now a mature technology; however there are still refinements and cost reductions to be had, especially in markets which have not until now installed many systems.

Obviously, the cost and effectiveness of solar water heating varies substantially with location. In India, in areas not subject to frost, the installed cost of a solar water heater is quite modest, energy capture is very high, and supplementary forms of water heating are unlikely to be required. In Alaska, one gets lots of hot water in summer, but very little in winter, and an expensive system to accommodate regular severe winter frosts is required.

## Solar Thermal Power

The majority of people think of solar thermal power, otherwise known as "concentrating solar power" (CSP) when they hear the phrase "solar thermal." This technology is an alternative way to generate power from the sun, and is applicable in areas with high levels of direct sunshine.

There are several ways to go about generating solar thermal power, the most common being parabolic trough, Fresnel reflector or lens, and central tower. There is also the possibility of using parabolic dishes with a central generator. With the exception of parabolic dishes, solar thermal power is almost always a large (utility) scale technology. All solar thermal power systems have in common the need to concentrate sunshine onto some kind of receiver in order to achieve high temperatures, which are then used to generate electricity using a turbine or reciprocating engine.

Recently, with huge reductions in the cost of photovoltaic power (PV), solar thermal has somewhat fallen out of favor as its cost of generation is now significantly higher than PV. This situation has, however, driven innovation so that a number of new approaches and refinements are set to bring down the cost of solar thermal power, potentially making it competitive once again.

It should be noted that the chief advantage of solar thermal power over PV is the ability, at a relatively modest cost, to add storage in the form of molten salts, phase change materials, or hot stone / concrete. For very high temperature applications, liquid glass is also under development. With storage, unlike PV, a solar thermal power station can operate in a dispatchable manner, regulating power output up or down according to need, and may generate power 24 hours a day. (An alternative way to achieve 24/7 generation is the use of hybrid technology – burning gas to run the turbines when the sun is not shining.)

Storage or hybridization makes solar thermal power much easier to install on an electrical grid at high penetration levels, and allows the generators to be used at far higher capacity factors than are possible for PV.

# Levers to Reduce the Cost of Solar Thermal Power

There are three major technical approaches to reducing the cost of solar thermal power.

1. Increased efficiency

   Increasing the efficiency of a solar thermal power station is an important lever for reducing the cost of power, and may be achieved by ensuring that the highest possible proportion of available heat is collected, and that the concentration level is as high as possible. The first part, improving efficiency by collecting a higher proportion of the available heat, has been almost exhausted now, with only small gains still available. However, increasing temperature by increasing concentration ratio (the thermal properties of available materials permitting), and focusing heat more accurately onto a smaller receiver, still has a way to go in terms of technology maturation. Increasing efficiency is therefore largely a matter of improving mirrors and collectors, and ensuring improved accuracy of solar tracking so that heat is not lost by poor alignment.

   Typically, parabolic trough collectors make steam at temperatures of 300C to 400C, limiting thermal generation efficiency to a theoretical maximum efficiency of around 49% at 300C, or 56% at 400C. (In reality, once temperature losses between the troughs and the turbine, mechanical losses, and generator losses are taken into account, actual efficiency is somewhat lower.) Were it possible to further increase temperatures to 500C without too much loss of heat by radiation or poor focusing, this would push theoretical efficiency up to a maximum of around 62%, or 26% more power generated per area than at 300C, all other things being equal.

Higher temperature operation reduces the amount of land needed per MW, cuts down on materials required, and reduces "soft costs" associated with the planning process. In the event that storage is used, this also allows for a smaller storage vessel per MWh stored, thus cutting the cost of energy storage.

2.  Reduce the cost of material inputs

Traditionally, mirrors used in solar thermal power plants have been made of glass. Precision curved glass is expensive, requires specialist manufacture, is heavy, and tends to be expensive and difficult to transport. More recently, alternative systems have been used based on curved steel or aluminum covered with an aluminized Mylar laminate on a bolt-together frame. This system is less expensive, allows the hardware to be packed more closely for transport further lowering costs, and enables a higher proportion of local manufacture.

Another alternative way to make mirrors using very low cost materials is to make parabolic troughs using cast concrete; a precise parabolic surface could then be achieved using 3D printing after which aluminized Mylar laminate can be applied, as would be the case for steel or aluminum laminate mirrors.

Rather than using mirrors, some solar thermal projects are beginning to use linear Fresnel reflectors or lenses to concentrate sunlight. Fresnel technology has the advantage of using flat or nearly flat components, so facilitating both mass production, and ease of transport, potentially eliminating a substantial chunk of the cost of a solar thermal system.

Lower cost storage – There are several drawbacks to the use of molten salt. Its use requires a heat exchanger to take heat from the molten salt to produce steam, and the salts cannot be allowed to cool below their freezing temperature at any time. This can be quite inconvenient, and any accidental freezing can result in substantial maintenance expenses. In addition, it will sometimes be necessary to expend energy from external sources to keep the salts liquid.

To overcome these problems, an Israeli company is proposing to use direct steam generation and a concrete-like storage medium buried below the troughs. In this system steam is both a heat transfer medium and the substance which expands in the turbines without the need for intermediate heat exchangers. This avoids the temperature losses that inevitably accompany the use of heat exchangers, thus improving system efficiency. The system also uses steam to heat up the "concrete" storage medium during the day to allow continued generation in the evening and night. The system is projected to achieve far lower energy storage costs than the current incumbent molten salt technology.

3. Reduce the cost of manufacturing

As with any technology, volume manufacture and a whole raft of usually small iterative changes has and will continue to cut the costs of solar thermal power while at the same time boosting efficiency.

The Sunshot Initiative has a cost target of 6 cents per kWh for solar thermal power by 2020, though this is rather demanding; the DoE CSP target is less demanding: 9 cents per kWh in 2020. Whether or not either of these targets can be achieved, it is nearly certain that costs will continue to fall, offering an even more attractive means of generating renewable electricity 24/7 in the sunny regions of the world.

## A Word of Caution

One technical concern about solar thermal power is the high-volume use of water. The desert areas of the world best suited to CSP are inherently short of water, and water-cooled steam turbines use a lot of water. It might be necessary to adopt air-cooling for many CSP projects, but this increases their capital costs and adversely affects their efficiency, delaying the date at which CSP becomes widely attractive on pure economic grounds without the use of subsidies or incentives.

# Chapter Five—
# Cheap Energy Storage

Storage will soon become quite inexpensive as well, as it provides numerous benefits to all concerns with electricity generation, transmission, distribution, and consumption. Having said that, the fact that everyone wins with storage has, ironically, functioned historically as a drawback, as it has forced us to answer a tough question: who pays for it, and how? However, for reasons provided below in the chapter on the re-regulation of the power utilities, we are quite close to having all this resolved.

Let's look at some of the challenges. Energy storage is virtually non-existent at this point. Pumped hydro represents over 98% of the total energy storage, but adding more is problematic, as there are severe siting and environmental issues associated with it.

It's hard to know what to make of batteries, especially given the false claims that have been made in the arena over the last 50 years. Even on their best day, there are environmental challenges associated with the entire lifecycle analysis surrounding each of the major battery chemistries: sourcing and shipping raw materials, construction, and disposal. There are also cycling issues, i.e., how many times a battery can be charged and discharged before significant performance degradation is experienced. In addition, we must deal with excess heat: for small batteries, say, in electric vehicles, this really doesn't pose a problem, but at the multi-megawatt scale, heat builds up and is hard to dissipate.

Synthetic fuels seek to use off-peak energy and a series of endothermic chemical processes that build liquid fuels (gasoline, diesel, and jet fuel) from the hydrogen in electrolyzed water and point sources of $CO_2$, like coal-fired power plants and cement manufacturing plants. Thus, these processes are carbon-neutral, meaning that we're returning the carbon into the atmosphere.

The challenge facing synthetic fuels is to pull all this off with some reasonable level of efficiency. Historically, such attempts have produced efficiencies between 20% and 30%, though it appears that these can be pushed northward of 60%, at which point the costs of such enterprises begin to become attractive.

If there is a concept here that has any real future, it's Doty WindFuels, a start-up based in Columbia, South Carolina, run by some of the brightest people on the planet. WindFuels is described in some depth in Part Three below.

Obviously, a better solution would be one that didn't deal with carbon in the first place. Compressed air energy storage (CAES) is such a solution, using depleted natural gas wells, salt domes, or even excavated rock formations as the repositories in which air can be pressurized with off-peak energy, and depressurized when needed.

Advanced rail energy storage (ARES) is another potential solution that has nothing to do with carbon. One should think of this as "pumped hydro without the hydro"; it's simply the concept of using off-peak energy to drive a motor and push a heavy mass on rails uphill, then allowing it to fall downhill and generate electricity when energy is needed.

The world is very close to realizing how valuable energy storage is—not only for its ability to capture electric energy that would otherwise be wasted, but for its ability to provide ancillary services, like the regulation of voltage and the AC wave form, problems that are becoming thornier as our grids grow larger and more complex. In the chapter on the power utilities, we also note that recent legislation is paving a path by which providers of these services can be adequately compensated.

The fossil fuel industry, in its efforts to suppress and delay the migration to clean energy, understands that the addition of storage is a huge enabler for renewables, and has historically done everything in its power to keep it from happening—largely by confusing those trying to make sense of it. In legal hearings on the matter, they insist that storage providers answer the question: Is storage a generation asset or a transmission asset? When those testifying point out that the question has no meaning, they're accused of being "disrespectful." Of course, those posing the question are well aware that there is no good answer; it's reminiscent of Salem in 1692 (Tell us: Are you a witch, or are you a sorceress?)

While it's true that we have previously thought of generation and transmission as distinct elements of our grid, this idea needs to be discarded in the context of energy in the 21st Century. Fortunately, the good guys are winning this debate; we appear to have reached the point where our judges are losing their patience for and tolerance of stonewalling in this arena.

## Ancillary Services

A number of European markets already have a market for grid regulation / ancillary services. In the UK, there is a company dedicated to aggregating these services from a large number of mid-sized suppliers, able to make power available to the grid at short notice. Mostly this takes the form of on-site combined heat and power (CHP) and standby generators coming on line or adjusting their output in response to signals from the National Grid (the operator of the UK's electricity grid).

## Demand Response

Other providers deliver this power by temporarily cutting consumption by switching off large scale refrigeration / air conditioning plants for an hour or two – relying on thermal inertia in large buildings and refrigerated warehouses to keep temperatures within the required range until the grid is more stable. In the future, large battery systems are likely to be added to the mix.

Many speculate as to what Google might have planned for the future, and among the speculations are ideas relating to disruptive technology in the electricity market, and how their acquisition of Nest might fit into these plans.

It's quite possible that Google (through Nest) might be planning for next-generation demand response. In some markets around the world, including the UK, Germany, and Denmark, there is an actively traded market for demand response services. These services are part of the process by which the electricity grid remains stable.

Traded demand response services include the following.

• Frequency response – The electricity grid is a very precisely tuned clock designed to run at exactly 60Hz in the U.S., and 50Hz in many other countries such as those of the European Union. The amount of tolerance allowed for frequency excursions is very low; in any given 24 hour period, the aim is to achieve precisely the same number of oscillations.

With conventional generators where generation occurs through rotation of a rotor with respect to a stator, the grid frequency is directly set by the aggregated speed of rotation of all the generators on the grid. The full picture is somewhat more complex, involving a degree of slip, rather like a clutch by which generators run slightly faster than required to generate the nominal frequency, and motors (which are effectively generators in reverse) slightly slower. The speed of rotation tends to rise if there is too much power on the grid, or slows if there is too little.

This being the case, keeping the "clock" precisely accurate requires moment-by-moment balancing of supply and demand. In fact, the grid frequency does vary very slightly so that on a 60Hz grid, there might be short periods of rapidly rising demand when the grid frequency drops to 59.9Hz, and other periods of rapidly falling demand where frequency rises to 60.1Hz. While this might be allowed for a few minutes, the grid operator will make strenuous efforts to balance out even the smallest deviations over the course of the day.

This is where frequency response comes in. Particularly on grids where there is a lot of intermittent generation such as Germany and Denmark, the sudden onset of a storm rapidly ramping wind power generation, or the rising of the sun on a summer morning can give rise to a very fast change in generation, which in extreme cases can be faster than the remaining generators can respond—leading to frequency deviations. These can be positive or negative, and the grid operators are willing to pay money to organizations that are able to ramp their electricity use up or down voluntarily to counter this effect. Examples of such organizations are water utilities who might switch water pumps on and off for a time at the request of the grid operator (they can almost always adjust the timing of water transfers between service reservoirs).

- Voltage Response – Whereas the entire power grid operates at one frequency, the same is not true of voltage. Allowable voltage excursions are quite large – with voltage in the EU being nominally 230V with a range of +10% and -6%. On any given power line, assuming that power flows one way from the local transformers to power users, voltage will drop according to the $I^2R$ law; the farther away you are from the supply, the more power is drawn along the way. With the addition of many locally distributed renewable generators, or unexpectedly heavy loads, there is the possibility of a local voltage deviation, often called an "excursion." Demand response suppliers will in this case adjust their power use to support balance in their local power supply. At times, there might possibly be a need to damp demand nationally while raising it on a particular local circuit.

- Phase balancing – Electricity is generated and distributed in three phases which need to be kept in balance. Typically, larger commercial users will receive a three-phase power supply while homes often receive only one phase, with homes on a given circuit taking turns to be connected to phases 1, 2 and 3. At any given moment, you will not have an exact balance between the power demand on the three phases, which can result in increased distribution losses. Some commercial users have the capability to split demand across the three phases to counter this imbalance across phases, which helps the grid operator to run an efficient system.

- Power factor and wave form correction – In an ideal world, each of the three electricity phases should deliver a pure sine wave AC power supply to every user with the three phases being separated by precisely 120 degrees. However, certain loads, such as capacitors and inductive loads, can cause a phase to lag or lead while other loads controlled by pulse width modulation can chop out bits of the wave form making the power supply "dirty" and likely to trigger faults in precision electronics.

There are solutions which can be applied which restore fully in phase clean sine wave operation. These too can be of commercial value and potentially bought and sold on traded markets.

## How Demand Response Is Traded

Currently, grid operators like to purchase demand response and other grid support services from a small number of very large users, each of whom is in a position to adjust its power use up or down by several megawatts on demand. In some markets such as the U.K. and Australia, aggregators operate entities such as Flextricity which target the "next rung down the ladder" of organizations with > 500 kW of demand flexibility. Even so, the number of players able to participate is very low compared to the total number of electricity users.

## How Nest Might Shake up the Demand Response Market

A clue to this comes in a master's degree thesis by John Barton of Loughborough University in the UK. He speculated as to how much "spinning reserve" might be made available by adjusting the operating instructions of every refrigerator and freezer in the country from domestic units in people's homes up to massive refrigerated warehouses. His premise is that while a domestic fridge is recommended to be kept between 2C and 6C, that the exact temperature of the fridge at any given time, provided it remains in range, is not important, and a fridge can be used to provide demand response by remotely adjusting the programming of its thermostat.

Suppose under ordinary circumstances, the fridge is programmed to turn on the compressor when the fridge reaches 5C and turn it off when the temperature drops to 3C, you can adjust when the fridge uses most power by moving this band up or down by 1 degree. E.g., if there is too much power on the system, start the compressor at 4C and turn off at 2C, in the opposite situation, the compressor remains off until the fridge reaches 6C and turns off at 4C. At all times, the fridge remains inside acceptable temperature limits, but it brings forward or defers power use – possibly by several hours.

This might not appear likely to make a significant difference, but John's paper gives an estimate of 1.5 GW of aggregated up or down regulation being achievable across the UK simply by applying such an adjustment across every refrigerating device in the land.

Aside from refrigerators and freezers, other appliances might be similarly controlled, with washing machines and dishwashers interrupting their wash cycles, water heaters timing their operation to suit the grid, air conditioning units allowing an extra degree of temperature flexibility, borehole pumps likewise, and electric cars adjusting their charging protocols to support grid stability. (This is by no means a complete list.)

With the Internet of Things, Nest offers the potential for every such device to become "smart," i.e., capable of adjusting its power use on demand, even if only by tens of watts. Collectively, all such devices add up to a colossal demand response supply capable of massively increasing the amount of intermittent renewable generation which can be integrated into the power grid while maintaining tighter control than is currently possible of frequency, of local voltage, and of phase balance – without the need to add expensive power storage.

This could be turned into cash in a number of ways, one concept for which is making a micro-payment of a fraction of a cent to the owner of each device, to be offset against the electricity bill, every time demand response is activated (much like pay per click advertising).

## More on Energy Storage

The most common traditional methods of energy storage are pumped hydro and lead acid batteries, both of which have limitations.

## Pumped Hydro

Traditionally, pumped hydro power storage has involved the construction of two hydro-electric dams one above the other in a single valley so that water leaving the top dam generates power before entering the lower dam. The process can then be reversed to store power by pumping water back up to the upper dam with a cycle efficiency that can reach 80%. Pumped hydro provides relatively low cost storage at large scale and with the capability of storing power for days, weeks, or even months. Such systems have a design life than can exceed 100 years.

The main limitations of pumped hydro are geography, and the availability of water, with many of the best sites already in use. The dams behind pumped hydro reservoirs can also flood large areas of land which has a cost both financially and environmentally.

There are two emerging variants of pumped hydro which help to overcome some of the geographical and water limitations of pumped hydro.

1.  Seawater pumped hydro

    With seawater pumped hydro, only one dam is needed with the sea acting as the lower storage reservoir. While dam construction costs are reduced, there is the need to ensure that sea water does not contaminate fresh water supplies, and to use marine grade pump turbines. There are a number of sites around the world where such an arrangement might be considered, such as in Northern Africa or the Arabian Gulf where it is fairly common for land to rise rapidly as you travel away from the sea.

Currently there is one demonstration sea water pumped hydro plant in Okinawa, Japan, which is rated at 30 MW, and a much larger one proposed for Glinsk in Ireland, to be rated at 1.5GW / 6 GWh which would allow the integration of a number of permitted but not yet constructed wind farms.

2. Closed Loop Pumped Hydro

There are proposals to build a number of closed loop pumped hydro systems in Australia and elsewhere. The main advantage of a closed loop system is that it does not need to be constructed on a river so removing a geographical constraint. The upper and lower reservoirs are connected to each other and the same water can be continually re-circulated, barring evaporative and leakage losses, so that the amount of water needed can be kept relatively low. Such systems can be constructed using deep reservoirs with small surface area, and further enhanced using covers or other techniques to minimize evaporation.

## Lead Acid Batteries

Lead acid batteries are a 100+ year old technology which have a low capital cost, and which can be efficiently recycled at the end of their lives. The downsides of lead acid technology are poor cycle life under deep cycle conditions, shortened life when the batteries get hot, moderate-to-high self-discharge, and low cycle efficiency of around 60% when charged and discharged quickly. Lead acid batteries are also heavy, thus limiting their effectiveness in transportation applications.

Lead acid batteries have traditionally been used with off-grid solar; however in hot climates batteries need replacement more often. In order to preserve cycle life, it is also necessary to over-specify capacity usually by a factor of approximately two.

The main modes of failure of lead acid batteries are sulphation where insoluble lead sulphate crystals grow, locking away part of the lead from taking part in the chemical reactions which power the battery, and substantially increasing internal resistance so reducing capacity, and cycle efficiency.

## Advanced Lead Acid

Advanced lead acid batteries overcome the life limiting traits of older forms of lead acid while simultaneously increasing cycle efficiency. Typically, these batteries use porous carbon electrodes rather than lead electrodes, so eliminating anode corrosion issues while the small pore size of the porous carbon limits the growth of lead sulphate crystals so that they remain small enough to dissolve. These batteries are slightly more expensive than traditional deep-cycle lead acid, however they can be 100% discharged without compromising their cycle life, and are rated at around 5,000 cycles of 100% discharge with typically 85% cycle efficiency, due to the high electrical conductivity of carbon electrodes.

Lifetime capital costs / kWh stored are far lower than they are for old-style deep-cycle batteries, and far less electricity is lost through cycling. For the moment, however, energy density remains low, although this is not a problem for static applications.

## The All-Liquid Battery

Professor Donald Sadoway of MIT and his team are developing an all-liquid battery consisting of lithium metal floating on a molten salt electrolyte which in turn floats on a liquid mix of lead and antimony. The battery runs at 500C, and self-stratifies to form the components of a battery. The technique is in effect the reverse of the process used for electrochemical extraction of aluminum from ore.

Unlike traditional batteries, there is no complex manufacturing process, and the size of individual cells is almost unlimited. This being the case, utility-scale batteries are likely to become possible using low cost bulk materials, thus offering an unprecedentedly low cost per kWh stored. Cycle efficiency is 73% at 275 milliamperes per square centimeter, and there is no obvious mode of battery deterioration other than for the containment vessel and associated electronic components.

## Isentropic

Isentropic is a UK company developing a new form of utility scale energy storage system involving two large sealed steel tanks filled with gravel, and an argon atmosphere. Argon is kept at atmospheric pressure in one tank, and at 12 bar in the other. Argon is pumped from the low pressure tank and compressed in a piston so that it becomes hot, and is discharged at the top of the high pressure gravel tank, heating the gravel. It is then released through a valve dropping the temperature in the second low pressure cold vessel. As a result of this process, the hot compressed argon can reach 500C before transferring its heat to the gravel while on the cold side, expanding argon can reach -160C, chilling the gravel in the cold tank. The process is then reversed to generate electricity with the hot gravel driving expansion of argon, and the cold gravel, its contraction.

Cycle efficiency is 72% to 80% and the system is designed for 2 to 5 MW of power for up to 8 hours.

The cost of this solution is expected to come in a little lower than pumped hydro, without the associated geographical constraints. Systems can therefore be placed either close to demand, or close to intermittent generation such as wind and solar farms allowing such facilities to deliver dispatchable power, and permitting transmission capacity to be less than the maximum output of the facility.

These are just a few of many approaches to reducing the cost of energy storage. Many others are under development such as secondary sodium ion, zinc nickel, zinc manganese and zinc air batteries. With so many new technologies under development, and existing technologies expanding so availing themselves of learning curve cost reductions, there is near certainty that substantial new energy storage capacity will emerge, and that this new capacity will have substantially lower costs and less restricted applications than the incumbent technologies.

# Chapter Six—
# Storage Isn't the Only Solution to the Variability of Solar and Wind

As we have seen, renewable electricity technologies are making rapid progress towards delivering power at a cost fully competitive with fossil fuels, a goal which has now been achieved in some markets in certain situations. Solar photovoltaic power in particular has seen a huge reduction in cost per installed watt sustained with some cyclical interruptions over several decades. It looks likely that solar power with already foreseeable technical and soft cost advancements can halve its generation costs from today's level in the U.S. market by 2020, so achieving the Sunshot goals of the National Renewable Energy Laboratory of utility scale solar installing for $1 per watt in the U.S.

Likewise for wind, the cost per kWh of power delivered in the U.S. has declined by 40% since 2004 when there was more demand for wind turbines than the industry could supply–this in spite of many of today's wind farm sites being in moderate- rather than high-wind locations. Innovations in turbine design have also enabled today's wind farms to achieve similar capacity factors to those of 10 years ago even though they sit in less windy areas.

Wind power is a more mature technology than solar, and inherently involves substantial material inputs; turbines are innately an example of heavy engineering. Foundations for the largest turbines weigh thousands of tons, while towers also need large quantities of steel or concrete, and top head mass, i.e., everything which is hauled up to the nacelle: generator, gearbox, drive shaft, and turbine blades can weigh several hundred tons. In addition, it is often necessary to build some kind of road structure to the turbines—even if it may not need a sealed surface.

The weight of a wind turbine per MW with all its support is a great deal higher than that for 1 MW of solar array, particularly if mounted on a commercial rooftop. This being the case, there would appear to be less scope for reducing the cost of onshore wind power than is possible for solar power.

Lowering the cost of intermittent sources of electricity is only part of the story. To achieve a true revolution in how we supply electricity, as well as a similar revolution in heat and other forms of energy, it is necessary to make energy available in the quantities required at the times when it is needed, rather than when it's generated. While there is a good correlation between generation and load for solar, the precise opposite is true for wind.

## The Challenge of Intermittency

Again, the two most frequently used forms of modern renewable energy are solar photovoltaic and wind power, both of which are by their nature intermittent.

Photovoltaic power (unless it is based in space--which has been proposed, but which is likely to prove excessively expensive) is inherently available for an average of at most 12 hours a day at any given location, so any power supply system heavily dependent on solar power will need to use another form of generation at night or store power for when it is needed. In addition, outside the tropics, day length varies significantly between summer and winter, and the amount of solar power which can be generated is further limited by varying weather conditions. In high latitudes, seasonal variation is a particular challenge as demand tends to be highest in winter when solar arrays produce relatively little power. For this reason, solar power in such areas is likely to be limited to a fairly modest proportion of total annual generation for the foreseeable future. (In Germany, solar power currently produces around 7% of annual electricity demand, peaking at over half of demand on sunny summer Sundays.)

Wind power likewise is intermittent and variable in its output, and while a wind turbine in a good location might well generate power for the vast majority of the time, the amount of power output will change from minute to minute with changes in the weather. Typically, in Europe, weather systems last around four days so that rather than the diurnal variation in solar power, hourly averaged wind power output tends to vary over a cycle of several days.

While wind and solar power form a small part of the overall power supply, they can be added to the grid with little impact on the operation of other power generators. Demand for electricity is inherently variable, so that existing systems are always designed with a degree of output flexibility to accommodate this. A few wind turbines, or modest solar farms can be accommodated by this existing flexibility. As solar and wind power generation increase to the point where they form a substantial part of a grid's overall supply, the challenges of balancing supply and demand become greater, and the need for a solution more urgent.

Hydro power is a third form of intermittent renewable, and it is one which tends to complement wind and solar power very well. Most hydro plants involve holding water behind a dam and releasing it through a generator as required. In most cases, it is not possible to operate at full capacity 24/7 as doing so would cause all the water behind the dam to be depleted. For this reason, hydro power is usually intermittent and variable in nature but with the important difference from wind and sun that the intermittency is dispatchable.

Given the dispatchable nature of hydro power it is the perfect balancing power source, able to defer generation when wind and sun are abundant or demand is low, then to ramp up output at short notice if the wind dies down or solar power suddenly decreases. In this way, wind and sun save water when they provide power which can be used later when wind and sun are not available in sufficient quantity.

It should be noted that for a large number of African countries, hydro power forms a very large proportion of the available power supply, which, in any case, falls far short of meeting all the demands of the people. This being the case, nearly every African country is in a position to integrate a significant amount of distributed widely dispersed wind and solar power balanced by their existing hydro power facilities.

The challenge of intermittent generation takes two forms.

- To balance supply and demand, it is very useful to be able to forecast both. A perfect forecast for either is inherently impossible; however extensive efforts are made to approximate the levels of supply and demand, and to schedule generation accordingly. With increasing intermittent generation, the absolute error in supply forecasting increases, and creates a greater demand for flexibility at short notice from those generators which can be flexible in their output. In turn, this tends to result in these flexible generators' operating outside their sweet spot at lower efficiencies than would normally be the case. The contribution of wind and solar power to the grid will always save fuel, but a portion of this gain will be lost to these lower efficiency operating modes of flexible generation. Improved forecasting can enable better scheduling of flexible generators so cutting the efficiency penalty of having large amounts of solar and wind power on the grid.

- Excess electricity production. At high penetration of intermittent generation, there is likely to arise from time to time a situation where supply exceeds demand within the local area requiring the use of either dump loads or "spilling" to keep the grid stable. "Spilling" means instructing solar or wind generators either to stop supplying power to the grid, or to reduce output by deliberately capturing less power than is available. An alternative is to export the power from the area if sufficient transmission capacity and a market for the power exists elsewhere. Denmark currently exports a large portion of its extensive wind power generation, and at times is unable to achieve a decent price for the power. In extreme cases, the spot market price for power has even gone negative.

## Solutions to Intermittency

Solutions to the challenges of intermittency take three generic forms which are as follows.

- Energy Storage. As covered in more detail in the chapter on this subject, when excess power is produced, or when it is desired to make delivery of power to the grid more predictable, a proportion of intermittent generation can be stored in some form or another. Storage technologies include a wide range of chemical batteries, pumped hydro, compressed air energy storage, mechanical storage using flywheels or heavy trains moving up and down hill, or thermal storage in the form of heat and cold which depending on their temperatures can be used either to generate electricity (as is the case with molten salts in concentrating solar thermal plants) or to produce thermal services such as space heating, cooling, and refrigeration. Storage is currently receiving a great deal of interest, with a large number of competing technologies racing to offer cost effective utility scale energy storage.

• Demand side management, meaning shifting the time of demand to better reflect the availability of power. Services like water pumping, preparation of separated gases (oxygen, nitrogen, $CO_2$, and Argon from air), ice-making, and some industrial processes can be timed to use low-value electricity, or to avoid peak demand times. New developments in the Internet of Things appear likely to offer an unprecedented level of demand response capacity from devices of all sizes adding greatly to the resilience of the grid, and to the amount of intermittent capacity which can be accommodated.

• Expanding the geographical spread of the grid. Europe is currently in the process of adding significant new transmission capacity between certain regions in order to move intermittent power to where it can more easily be used, for example, from the northwest of Germany to Bavaria in the south, between the U.K. and Ireland, between the U.K. and France, as well as a proposed interconnection between Iceland, the U.K. and Norway. There are also plans for an offshore European supergrid to connect all the countries along the Atlantic and North Sea coasts of Europe as well as Morocco.

This geographical spread is wider than typical weather systems, thus enabling a windy day in Morocco to offset low wind power production in Northern Europe. This aggregation reduces the amount of supply variation in relation to the overall demand, and reduces the percentage error on supply output estimates for intermittent generators. Similar grid reinforcement and expansion is occurring in a number of geographical regions.

# Chapter Seven—
# All Other "Flavors" of Renewable Energy Are Making Progress Too

Biomass, geothermal, ocean thermal and hydrokinetics are all making key contributions. This is important, as there are parts of the world that have an amazing abundance of these resources, while lacking others.

For instance, consider Nepal, which (sadly) is experiencing rapid growth due to the explosion of tourism. Fortunately, with the most abundant hydro resources on Earth, there will be no reason to burn a molecule of hydrocarbons to meet this demand.

As well as having huge hydro power resources which have the potential to deliver more power than the country can use, Nepal has superb solar resources which are ideal for delivering power to smaller more remote communities where grid connection is not cost effective, and where micro-hydro is not an option. Solar is an excellent solution for small off-grid communities as it is highly scalable from a few watts all the way up to solar farms of many megawatts, and solar technology also offers highly cost-effective water heating. Likewise wind resources are excellent in some parts of the country. This being the case, Nepal is in an ideal position to deliver all its energy needs from sustainable resources. With the cost of solar and wind technology, as well as that of battery storage for small off grid systems dropping rapidly, there is scope for rapid and cost effective delivery of electricity at all scales both on and off the grid.

Similarly, consider Iceland. What they lack in solar resources they more than make up for in geothermal, as well as hydro power and potential for wind power. Today, Iceland generates virtually all its power from geothermal and hydro resources and heats nearly all its buildings using geothermal heat. Even so, there is vast potential to further increase power production way beyond what could be utilized by Iceland's 320,000 people - so much so that there have been talks between Iceland, the UK and Norway about building a 5 GW interconnecting cable to enable the large scale export of Icelandic geothermal power to the European market while simultaneously building a major link in the European Super-grid enabling substantially increased international trade in electricity, and supporting geographically dispersed renewable generation.

Geothermal and hydro-power costs in Iceland are low, and large businesses are reportedly signing 20-year fixed-price power contracts for as little as $0.04 per kWh, and energy intensive businesses like aluminum production and data centers, which in Iceland's cold climate require very little cooling, are attracted as a result.

Iceland's theoretical geothermal capacity is around 12 GW, and that was before the possibility of using magma to generate very high temperature steam was taken into account, something that was accidentally achieved in 2009.

Then consider what we can do for the more than one billion people living near the coastlines that are within 1000 miles of the equator, who, if they have had any electrical power at all, have been generating it from imported bunker diesel, which is extremely expensive, incredibly dirty, and posed enormous risks to national security. Now technologists have developed "ocean thermal energy conversion," an affordable way to extract the heat from the warm waters that occupy the top few meters of these tropical oceans. Readers will find more on this subject in Part Three, below.

Here's a fairly detailed section on the ever-falling costs of geothermal. Readers who find this to be "TMI" (as a friend of mine likes to say, i.e., "Too Much Information) are welcome to skip ahead.

## Reducing the Cost of Geothermal Energy

Geothermal energy takes several different forms with a range of different applications. In all cases, heat is extracted from the Earth's crust where temperatures rise with increasing depth. In some areas, hot rocks are found closer to the surface than others, however high temperatures are present everywhere at sufficient depth.

The main sub-divisions of geothermal energy are:

- High Pressure Steam – This is the classic form of geothermal power in which a well is drilled down into a natural reservoir of high pressure steam. This form of geothermal power was first exploited in 1904. Such reservoirs are comparatively rare. Many more areas exist with hot rocks at accessible depths but which are either not fractured enough to release significant quantities of steam, or too dry to produce steam.

- Enhanced Geothermal – Similar to the above but requires hydraulic fracturing to create a suitable heat exchanger. Many more areas offer potential for enhanced geothermal than for classic geothermal power, and such resources are increasingly being exploited for power generation.

- Hot Dry Rocks – There are areas with accessible heat but with rocks too dry to make steam. Such rocks will usually also require hydraulic fracturing to provide a viable heat exchanger, after which water will have to be injected through one well, and extracted through one or more extraction wells. This process will require large amounts of water limiting the areas where it might be considered.

Usually water will be the heat exchange medium of choice, though $CO_2$ has been proposed as an alternative with the advantage that some of the $CO_2$ is likely to be captured and stored by the rock, thus removing it from the atmosphere. Hot dry rocks have not yet been exploited very much for power, but R & D is ongoing with a view to open up very substantial areas which are not suitable for other forms of geothermal power.

There are also different ways in which the heat can be extracted and used – direct high temperature steam, indirect with a binary cycle in which a mix of water and ammonia is heated via a heat exchanger by geo-thermally heated water. This mix of water and ammonia improves system efficiency where temperatures are relatively low. Indirect systems are also used where dissolved solids are too high to pass through a steam turbine without causing damage.

Both of these forms of geothermal are primarily used for electricity generation, though in some cases they provide energy for space heating or industrial processes. There is also the possibility to use low-temperature geo-thermal heat for space heating only - particularly where district heating systems exist. Virtually the whole of Iceland's buildings are heated by geothermal heat, and geothermal district heating is exploited in many countries, even including a few areas in the UK, which is not usually very geologically active.

Finally, there is a common confusion between ground source heat pumps and geothermal heat – particularly in the US, where in most cases heat pumps extract solar heat stored in the soil – temperatures are usually fairly stable through the year once one gets a few meters below ground.

It should be noted that geothermal energy differs from most renewable energy technologies in that there are no issues of intermittency of resource; geothermal power is regarded as firm baseload power with near zero $CO_2$ emissions.

## Where Costs Can be Taken out of Geothermal Energy

- Less unproductive wells. As with oil and gas, not every geo-thermal well that is drilled delivers viable geothermal heat. In some cases, the rock is harder, dryer, less fractured, more difficult to fracture, or contains more dissolved salts / more toxic salts than expected so that geothermal yield is lower than expected or non-existent from a commercial point of view, or too expensive to exploit. With each well costing on the order of $5 million to drill and prepare, and around half failing, avoiding un-productive drilling is an important means of reducing financial risk, reducing both intrinsic costs and the risk premium which is applied to geothermal drilling.

- ISOR (Iceland Geo-survey) is running a program called IMAGE (Integrated Methods for Advanced Geothermal Exploration). The program has three main pillars.

a.  Understanding the processes and properties that control the spatial distribution of critical exploration parameters at European to local scales. The focus will be on the prediction of temperatures, in-situ stresses, fracture permeability and hazards which can be deduced from field analogues, public data sets, predictive models and remote constraints. It provides rock property catalogues for b and c.

b.  Radically improving well established exploration techniques for imaging, detection and testing of novel geological, geophysical and geo-chemical methods to provide reliable information on critical subsurface exploration parameters. Methods include:

    i.   Geophysical techniques such as ambient seismic noise correlation and magnetotellurics with improved noise filtering,

    ii.  Fibre-optic down-hole logging tools to assess subsurface structure, temperature and physical rock properties,

    iii. The development of new tracers and geo-thermometers.

c.  Demonstration of the added value of an integrated and multidisciplinary approach for site characterization and well-siting, based on conceptual advances, improved models/parameters and exploration techniques developed as described in the bullet points above. Further, it provides recommendations for a standardized European protocol for resource assessment and supporting models.

If the program achieves its aims, well positioning will to a large degree be optimized so that a far higher proportion of wells will be productive. This in turn will cut prospecting costs and prospecting risk drawing more investment into the industry at lower financing cost.

- Better more cost effective hydraulic fracturing methods – In recent years, a huge number of oil and gas sites have been made productive by hydraulic fracturing, the processes of which have been steadily refined by industry. This experience has improved the technology and cut the costs of the process substantially, and can potentially be transferred to the geothermal industry. Many failed wells drilled in the hope of extracting high pressure steam can be given a second opportunity to succeed if a suitable rock "heat exchanger" can be engineered using hydraulic fracking technology, thus reducing cost and increasing the proportion of successful wells. The technique can also be applied in areas with sufficient heat but insufficiently fractured rock for geothermal power generation. Hydraulic fracking for geothermal heat extraction is now technically and economically feasible in some areas where this was not previously the case, and with further technological developments and learning curve, the zones where the process is viable can only get larger.

  Against geothermal fracking there is the issue of water availability – with some of the best geothermal regions also among the driest.

- New drilling techniques – drilling for oil or gas has certain key differences from drilling for heat. Typically, the former will involve drilling through relatively soft sedimentary rock to a moderate depth at which point the drill might well be directed horizontally along a productive seam of rock. By contrast, with geothermal, the steepest geothermal gradients are typically found in volcanic rocks such as granite and basalt which are typically much harder. This greatly increases drill bit wear and tear. To complicate matters further, geothermal drilling becomes more productive the deeper it goes particularly in regions with modest thermal gradients. Typically for very deep wells, the cost of drilling increases more or less exponentially with depth so that doubling drilling depth might well increase cost by a factor of 5 to 10 times. This greatly increased cost is largely based on two factors – increasing pressure with depth, and increases in the time required to extract and change worn drill bits. To exploit geothermal power in these less obvious areas, it would be highly desirable to be able to drill very deep wells at an affordable cost.

A number of techniques are under development in which non-contact drilling techniques substitute for a rotating drill bit. These include plasma drilling using a plasma torch to disintegrate rock at the base of the well. This technique is more energy efficient than rotary drilling for deep wells, allows constant operation without having to extract and change drill bits, enabling a casing of constant diameter, and offers effective transportation options for the disintegrated rock. Other variants of non-contact drilling techniques under development include water jet, hydrothermal spallation (fracturing the rock using thermal shock) and laser. Using these techniques, it is believed that deep drilling can be substantially speeded up with drilling cost coming much closer to linear with depth.

A combination of improved prospecting tools, better hydraulic fracturing techniques, and enhanced deep drilling technologies could potentially make geothermal power viable anywhere on the Earth's surface, so allowing geothermal power to deliver a large contribution to the future global energy mix. For this reason, it could be argued that geothermal power deserves a far higher profile and a greater amount of investment in basic research and development of advanced techniques than it currently receives.

# Chapter Eight—
# Other Important Macro-Economic Issues

## Costs Are Becoming Predictable

The cost of energy from fossil fuels depends on the cost of the fuels themselves, which fluctuates according to market pressures, and we've seen extreme volatility over the past few decades. By contrast, not only are renewable resources free, but perhaps best of all, that can't change; there will never be a cost associated with absorbing energy from sunlight or the wind (at least, we all need to hope that's the case). Not only does this concept of free fuel bring peace of mind, it saves a ton of money associated with hedges, purchasing futures, etc.

Volatility has a cost; when energy prices rise steeply, this can have an adverse impact on the economy, where sudden changes can destabilize energy producers. When prices change rapidly first in one direction then in the opposite direction, the volatility imposes additional costs on the economy by impacting planning, increasing hedging costs, and giving rise to resource allocation that in retrospect is inappropriate. To take a common example, airlines may expand their operations, but when oil prices suddenly rise they find that with the higher priced ticket, fewer seats are sold, and those are sold at a lower or even a negative margin.

Diversification of energy sources and the increased use of energy resources with fixed known costs have a hedging effect that provides value by reducing the overall size of energy cost-swings. This has already been seen in Europe, particularly in Germany, where one of the major effects of solar and wind power has been to reduce wholesale power prices.

With solar and wind power, the vast majority of costs are paid up front with comparatively low O&M costs (and no fuel cost). While power production is intermittent, the amount of power which can be expected per annum is fairly predictable. Once the initial payment has been made and financed, the cost of power is more or less fixed and not subject to the volatility of fuel prices. Once the capital cost is paid off, the cost of power from these resources for the remainder of their operational life (for as long as maintenance demands remain modest) is lower than can be achieved by any other technology.

## Economy of Scale

Market demand will soon reach the point that economies of scale will kick in.

The world power consumption is at 15 terawatts, and will double by 2050, driven chiefly by large urbanizing populations in Asia. Even with efficiency solutions, we'll need to generate at least an order of magnitude more power from renewable sources than we do now, and this will reduce costs per kilowatt-hour even further. In short, the demand for clean energy is about to skyrocket, at the same time the cost of producing it makes it affordable to all.

# Chapter Nine—
# The Upheaval of the
# Power Utilities

Recall what we said earlier about the unforecasted migration to cell phones about a decade ago, and how embarrassing this must have been for the market luminaries who missed the boat so badly. The difference here, however, is regulation; where the regulation that governed telephony was essentially gone by the mid-1990s, energy is extremely highly regulated, and we need to keep in mind that utility regulation happens at many different levels; in the U.S., it doesn't even necessarily happen at the state level; some states have more than one PUC (public utilities commission).

Fortunately, there is enormous pressure to reregulate and reorganize the power utilities, insofar as we realize that the utility environment is actively antagonistic to innovation—or change of any sort. Of course, this is not their fault; they are doing precisely what we ordered them to do when we created them in the early 20th Century. We told them we wanted cheap and reliable power, that we'd pay them a reasonable profit for doing that, that we wanted them to do exactly nothing else, and that's precisely what we got.

Now, of course, we're changing our minds; we need them to support the elements that will lower the footprint of energy: aggressive renewable portfolio standards, net-metering / distributed generation, energy storage, smart grid (including smart meters and appliances), long-distance high-voltage power transmission, demand response, and energy efficiency. In my opinion, it's not asking too much to allow us citizens to review the situation and make corrections every century or so. As readers will see in this chapter, there are numerous other issues affecting our utilities, making this an even more complex arena than it's ever been.

There are a great number of pressures that come to bear here, e.g.,

- Though it would be improper to say that Hurricane Sandy was a "fortunate" event, the grid resiliency issue it brought to the fore was most certainly the catalyst for re-regulating the utilities in New York and New Jersey.

- Fortunately, this is an important point of focus for NREL, which is hard at work analyzing the effect of things like rooftop solar and other forms of distributed generation, as well as a number of different forces that the modern world brings upon the utilities, like control of appliances with smart-phones.

- The Federal Energy Regulatory Commission (FERC) declared that compensation for use of assets needs to be fair. Though this concept received intense legal challenge, FERC's position was upheld by a U.S. Supreme Court ruling.

## Death Spiral

Many utility customers, both consumers and businesses, are breaking away from the grid in favor of distributed generation, thus increasing the costs for those who remain, which in turn provides even more incentive for customers to leave in ever-increasing numbers. Utilities are finding that they need to take radical action to deal with the so-called "death spiral."

While the death spiral is one possible narrative, there are other possible outcomes depending largely on the political decisions made by local, state, and federal authorities, as well as strategic business decisions made by the incumbent utilities. While it is technically possible for customers in some areas of the U.S. – particularly the southern states and Hawaii to go off-grid, it is likely that there will always remain an advantage in most locations to pooling generation resources from different locations, and across a range of technologies. (The cost of installing sufficient generation and electricity storage capacity to deliver enough electricity 24/7 without interruption is likely always to be higher than that of sharing the task with other users where a grid already exists). This being the case, it seems likely that utilities will gradually grow to resemble "broadband providers rather than fixed-line telephone services."

Up to this point, utilities have been in a powerful controlling position, starting off with a monopoly which has in many cases only partially been dismantled. In this way, utilities have been able to act like monopoly electricity providers, deciding if, when, and where to commission new generation facilities with a guaranteed return on their investments, and only offering a limited amount of opportunities for competing generation by other suppliers. Such utilities act somewhat like telephone providers, making most of their money from selling electricity – with their profits largely dependent on the volume of electricity sold. Technically speaking, the grid lends itself to remaining a monopoly, providing that there is a well-run market, and there can be any number of electricity and providers of grid balancing services.

The advancement of distributed generation, particularly solar, begins to challenge the monopoly, as a large proportion of the utility's customer base have at least the potential to deliver a significant proportion of their own generation, cutting into the market available to the existing utility. This is further compounded by the introduction and increasingly rapid deployment of more efficient technologies such as LED lighting which in many developed countries are already causing a year-by-year reduction in electricity consumption, thus reducing the overall size of the pie.

In the future, rather than being monopoly or near-monopoly electricity suppliers, it is possible that the utilities will evolve into service providers, effectively selling access to the grid (a natural technical monopoly), and managing the market for electricity services. In this way, each customer will pay a service charge for access to the grid and have the opportunity to both buy and sell services in the market place. Within the market, there will be opportunity to:

- buy or sell via power purchase agreements at a fixed price

- buy or sell on the spot market where prices vary hour by hour, or even minute by minute, or

- offer grid support services such as up and down regulation, phase balancing, voltage support, etc.

This has the potential to make the grid even more stable, balanced, and efficient.

In this scenario, the role of the utility would be to sell grid connection, rather like a broadband supplier selling a connection of a given size for a given price. Utilities could also be likened to a stock exchange, offering a marketplace for electrical services, earning a regulated spread margin on each transaction. In addition, the utility could offer supplementary services such as energy efficiency consultancy for businesses, and "breakdown insurance" for customer appliances.

It is possible that the utilities will split their businesses into, on the one hand, utility service companies, and on the other, independent generators competing in the marketplace. The utility in this situation will be far less dependent for its profits on the volume and price of electricity, and far more on efficiently providing grid services, delivering a well-run market, and efficiently managing the customer billing process for those who remain with them rather than buying their electricity from competing aggregators.

There is also the possibility for the authorities to set renewable obligations for a given portion of generation, and for there to be a requirement to deliver energy efficiency targets across their customer base, with levies on electricity bills set to cover the cost of these obligations, and sanctions on the utility should it fail to deliver.

While the above alternative to the death spiral will be highly dynamic, it is probable that individual users will buy their services from competing aggregators and so will see little difference in the way they are supplied and billed for electricity. The above utility model largely describes how the privatized competitive electricity market operates in the UK, with similar systems operating in a number of other EU markets.

*Enter Peter Fox-Penner*

In my estimation, Peter Fox-Penner is the brightest and most insightful electrical utility analyst on the planet. Rather than try to paraphrase his writings, I think I'll just provide a transcript of a short interview I had with him, and suggest that readers get a copy of his book, "Smart Power."

As my colleague Jigar Shah told be recently during a talk which I also present below, "Fox-Penner wrote the book on the subject – literally."

Craig: I want to ask you about the power utilities, how we're changing what we're asking of them, and how they're responding to all this. An obvious feature of this is their pushback on net-metering.

Peter: We regulated the utilities 100 years ago to prohibit them from getting richer than we wanted them to get. They earn only what we allow them to earn. Re: net metering, it's fundamentally unfair to low-income customers; it has an impact on rates. The utilities are not happy about losing sales, but also not happy about having to backfill and guarantee service to low-income customers when competitors who aren't regulated get skim off their high-end customers.

Technological change created the original utility compact about a century ago, and technological change is now requiring us to create a new utility compact over the next 30 or 40 years ago, while the grid is still around during this transitional period. The original compact was built around the grid being the only way to deliver power, and that's no longer the case.

CS: I would say that this is rooted in the fact that 100 years ago, we said that all we want is cheap and reliable power, and now we're realizing that we have an environmental problem, and so we're making a significant change in our demands.

PFP: That's only part of it. If the only problem we were facing vis-à-vis our relationship with the utilities were taking fossil fuels out of our electrical system, we could do that. We can build large scale solar facilities. We *are* building large-scale wind facilities, and they're getting less expensive every year. If decarbonization were the only issue, it wouldn't be a problem; we would not need to put PV on rooftops and go to distributed generation in its various forms.

But there are other drivers, and it's the combination of these specific drivers that creates the need for a new compact.

CS: How interesting. Take me through, that, please.

PFP: Well, the first one is flattening of sales growth. Electric utility growth, particularly in grid-supplied power is below one percent and is actually falling now in many areas. Companies, especially companies like these, don't do well unless they're growing. There are very few steady-state businesses out there.

CS: This is due to efficiency?

PFP: Yes, and there are many forms of efficiency, and the combination of them is really impactful. You have codes and standards in government policies, you have price-driven efficiency, and you have plain technology-based efficiency; it's a triple whammy on electric load growth.

The smart grid is a giant change, people can control their power; the technical relationships between electricity generation and customers can be much more sophisticated and complex than simply flipping a switch whenever you need power. The grid was built around the simple control notion that was: flip a switch and we'll give you all the power you need. So, smart grid is gigantically impactful, just like low load growth.

The third driver is distributed generation. While it's still more expensive than utility scale power, the costs are coming down enough that they are becoming cost-effective options for some customers.

CS: So, as a person of conscience, are you saying that, since we need a grid right now, we need to support it, so as to serve customers of all socio-economic classes?

PFP: I'm saying that, as what I hope is a person of conscience, is that a) getting as much carbon out of the energy mix as quickly as possible, b) achieving the other environmental goals besides carbon, and c) maintaining affordable and universal electric service—are all essential. When you put all these together, there is a role for rooftop PV and other distributed resources as well as grid-supplied power. My goal is to find the fastest path that meets all those objectives.

CS: I'm with you all the way there, but what would you say that path consists of?

PFP: It requires one of these new business models, with associated new government regulation, and the new ecosystem that results from it.

There are two business models / regulatory models / ecosystems that go with it, and they embrace the full suite of technologies that we see present, but in different amounts; I can't give you the exact breakdown.

CS: I hear you, but in essence, it sounds like you eventually have to conclude that rooftop solar is a bad thing—and I've heard other consumer advocates say the same thing. Utility-generated energy costs less now, and it always will. Sure, rich people can leave the grid, just like rich people can leave the public school system and form charter schools, or send their kids to private schools, but skimming the cream like this leaves a more degraded experience for the families who can't afford to leave. I.e., sure, we can do that, but we're building an elitist society where the rich get richer and the poor get poorer.

PFP: I do think the analogy you raise there has some useful merit, but I wrote the book to try to get away from the polarization between distributed vs. utility generation, and to avoid the dynamic you point out in public education.

We need to keep decarbonization moving as quickly as possible without losing the other objectives, which include affordable, universal service.

CS: OK, you mention that there are several of these "ecosystems," to use your word, that serve all these masters. Could you just take one and walk my readers through it, so they have a sense for what you're actually describing?

PFP: Sure. One of the business models / regulatory models / ecosystems in the book I call the "smart integrator." In the New York Rev (Reforming the Energy Vision) Proceedings, it's called Distribution Services Platform Provider, or DSPP. The idea is that it's an open-access, regulated utility entity; it operates an open-access distribution services platform. It sets prices for all the services it provides to the users of that platform. The platform consists of the physical distribution system for electrical energy, but also all the information services that go with it, e.g., information and system control, and load control services. That platform is open to the marketplace or ecosystem of energy efficiency providers, commodity electron retailers, solar installers, demand response providers, renewable energy providers, etc., who use some of the services from this platform, whether that's dispatching customer loads, which means changing how your load takes power through the platform, or how you inject your power into the distribution system—all of the services you use from the platform operate under tariff rates. It's open access, and operating something like that, and regulating something like that, and making sure that that entity is effective and efficient and serves the needs of all its users—that's the mission of the "smart integrator."

CS: Wow. And that's only one of two major ways of looking at the future of power utilities.

PFP: Yes, the other big concept is called "energy services utility." There, you continue to have a vertically integrated utility that continues to provide both commodity electrons and distribution services, and you still have about 30 of the U.S. states and much, though not all, of the rest of the world. But that model evolves into what I call an "energy services utility," and that entity must still operate a distribution services platform, but rather than operate it on an open-access, competitive, arms-length basis, it forms trusted partner-type relationships with the ecosystem and is in effect a bulk buying agent for its franchise customers, buying the same ecosystem services as are in the "smart integrator" model, buying them from the same entities competitively, but buying them as an aggregation agent.

CS: Wow. I study this stuff at some level, and I'm having trouble following every word you're saying. You must have the devil's own time trying to make yourself understood at cocktail parties.

PFP: That's true, Craig, and it's why I wrote the book. It's all laid out very simply and briefly; it's a one-airplane-ride read.

CS: I'll definitely check that out. Thanks very much.

*... And Here Comes Jigar Shah*

Here's a bit more on the subject, based on a call I had recently with a colleague: renewable energy entrepreneur Jigar Shah. Jigar plays an important role in New York's "Reforming the Energy Vision" (REV), which aims to encourage system efficiency with initiatives that will change the way electricity is distributed and used in New York State; it's an effort to scale up the clean energy economy and create a more resilient, clean, cost-effective and dynamic energy system.

I asked Jigar to walk me through the whole process by which we're changing our relationship with our utilities, and, as we'll see in the transcript here, he began with a bit of history.

Craig:   When we created the utilities, we said we wanted affordable and reliable power.  Now we're adding new conditions, and this is creating havoc.  What's happening here?

Jigar:   When we gave the utilities the mandate to provide electricity to everyone, and to do so by raising private capital, we gave them a monopoly, so as to make it easy for them on Wall Street—and even then, it wasn't that easy to do.  And the affordable piece didn't come in at the time; we directed them to give us electricity at any price.

Then we went through a period of reducing costs and improving reliability.  In the 1970s, we had so many blackouts and brownouts that we had to create the National Electric Reliability Council (NERC).  Over the next 30 years, from 1970 to 2000, NERC made sure they made all the required investments, e.g., building all these coal plants, so we could maintain that reliability.  Utilities hadn't really achieved reliable power until the latter part of the 20th Century.

At that point, we said that we wanted there to be competition; now that you've figured out how to do this reliably, we want competition to drive down prices.  Now, in the 21st Century, we have decarbonization, but actually, that wasn't the thing so much as diversification so as to get away from the volatility in natural gas prices. If you look at the renewable energy portfolio standards and why they were passed, it wasn't to promote renewable energy, but rather to diversify away from natural gas price volatility. In 2001, you'll recall that California had an energy crisis, where the price of natural gas went up, down, up, down, and so we installed more diversity into the mix to deal with that volatility.

Next, technology got so good that we would generate power for a customer like Walmart cheaper than Walmart could buy it from the utility. It had always been the case that electricity was priced such that, unless you were an industrial customer using 1000 megawatts, you could not self-generate power cheaper than the utility could sell it to you. But that crossover point happened in the last decade. And so, once we were past that crossover point, entrepreneurs like me went around the country, strategically picking out customers to serve. And that phenomenon, which was annoying to the utilities in 2003, is now in full force; it's causing enormous instability within the utility revenue model.

CS: Yes, the so-called "utility death-spiral."

I hear that New York is taking a very progressive tack here. Please tell me what they're doing.

JS: I would say that what New York is doing is conservative, not progressive. They're saying that the customer should be at the center of the universe. They want a system such that the customer can benefit from any and all innovation, and the utilities have to respond positively to that innovation, but still maintain the reliability of the grid.

CS: Well, I suppose it's a matter of semantics, but if you're saying that the customer gets all the upside of innovation, but the utility bears all the costs and risks, I would have called that progressive.

JS: Well, it's why what I'm doing with the NY public service program and NYSERDA (New York State Energy Research and Development Authority) is working so well: the entire Tea Party is behind me. Progressives are split 50-50, because half of them say I'm hurting poor people. Progressives like large government agencies or government-regulated agencies that protect poor people, and that's essentially what utilities do.

CS: I see.

The theme of the book is that market forces are in the process of ushering in renewable energy—regardless of our sensibilities vis-à-vis the environment.

JS: Yes, I subscribe to that.

CS: OK, given that, what's happening in the world of utility regulation that will either tend to accelerate that, or put the kibosh on it?

JS: "Utility 1.0" relied a lot on labor, metal, and concrete, all of which are really expensive compared with 1970 when they built all this stuff. If you wanted to stick with Utility 1.0 and wanted to replace old stuff with new stuff, you would basically double electricity rates in this country. The reason that we're winning with renewable energy—and I'm including now energy efficiency, demand response, load control, battery storage, etc.—is that we're the only way to accomplish this transition from old stuff to new stuff for less money. If you're a public regulator and your job is to keep rates low, you have to listen to us, because listening to the utility is going to get you fired.

In California, utility rates are going up about 5% per year, which is three times the rate of inflation. Social Security is indexed to the CPI, and so grandmothers are spending an ever-increasing portion of their monthly checks on electricity.

CS: So distributed generation is the only way for them to accomplish what they need to?

JS: That's right. And that's why we've had so much success—uniformly, from Georgia, Mississippi, Texas, Maryland, to Minnesota—we've been winning. It's the only way to not get fired—and to avoid having the governor who appointed you fired.

What makes this interesting is that in almost all states, utilities are by far the largest contributors to state and local political races, e.g., city council, state legislature, governors. So they have a lot of really powerful friends. But the reason they're losing this battle is that literally everyone else is against them: the American Lung Association, AARP, the Tea Party, the Sierra Club—every one of these people has a different reason to hate the utilities and to support renewables. They're all aligned around renewables, but each one for a different reason.

CS: Wow. Fascinating stuff. Thanks very much.

# Chapter Ten—
# Extremely Wealthy Forces of Super-Innovation Will Not Let 20th Century Energy Policy Slowly Destroy the Planet

Again, this chapter doesn't contain one iota of altruism. Yes, we'd like to think that young multibillionaires like Elon Musk and Mark Zuckerberg care more about the quality of the planet that we will leaving to posterity than certain other billionaires like David and Charles Koch. Maybe we're right, but in truth, it doesn't matter.

In any case, here's a short summary of what some of the major players seem to be thinking and doing.

# Google

Google is currently working towards 100% renewable energy sourcing for all its business activities; currently 34% of Google's energy comes from renewable sources. The company sees this as generating both environmental benefits and business opportunities, as well as enhancing the status and image of the company.

Google continues to seek out ways to source a higher proportion of renewable energy, and continues to pilot new clean technologies on its campuses. They perceive this, as a good investment as future running costs are reduced, and also as an opportunity to prove and scale new technologies. A cash-rich company sitting on $48.1 billion, Google is easily able to finance renewable energy developments such as wind and solar farms in a very cost-effective manner by signing highly bankable long-term power purchase agreements with developers, who can then use the PPA as collateral to fund the project. Google has also directly committed over $1 billion to finance wind and solar projects, and has achieved LEED status for over 2.5 million square feet of buildings.

In addition to the mostly mainstream renewable and energy efficiency measures discussed above, Google is also making strategic investments in a range of pre-commercial developments aimed at facilitating a greener energy future through acquisitions, and through offering prizes for strategically important breakthroughs.

- Makani Power – this company Google recently acquired is developing flying wind power technology in the form of tethered gliders propelled by the wind rather like a kite, and which generate power with propeller-driven generators as the glider tacks across the wind. This power is returned to the ground via a power cable in the tether. The product operates several hundred meters above ground, where wind power density is far higher than is experienced by conventional wind turbines, allowing them to operate at higher capacity factors (average power / nominal power capacity) than conventional wind.

Bill of materials per MW of generation has the potential to be far lower, as the device consists of a small launch tower and a lightweight flying wing; there is no need for hundreds or even thousands of tons of concrete tower and foundations. The system employs much smaller, faster rotating turbine blades, and smaller generators without the need for a complex and heavy gear box. Installation can be rapid and simple, potentially allowing deployment to support disaster recovery after which the device can quickly be moved to another site if required.

- Nest – Google invested $3.2 billion to purchase home energy management startup Nest. Among other things, Nest is working on smart home technology that is capable of deciding, among other things, when to run power-consuming devices and when to charge an electric car. Such technology can facilitate the integration of domestic and commercial building solar arrays by using power when it is most readily available, and limiting the export of power to the grid. This sort of technology will become more important over time as a higher proportion of generation is intermittent, and the challenges of keeping supply and demand in balance continues to grow. When washing machines, dish washers, water heaters, and electric car chargers become smart, it becomes possible to run them preferentially when intermittent power generation is high, or when other power uses are at a minimum, thus cutting the amount of conventional power generation (which tends to be most efficient running at around 75% of nominal capacity) operating on standby or at sub-optimal efficiency.

- The Little Box Challenge – this is a competition with a $1 million prize fund to develop smaller inverters. Inverters are found in many places such as solar arrays, wind turbines, electric vehicles and charging points, air conditioning units and many more. Smaller, lighter, and ideally more efficient inverters are very useful in bringing down costs, and in the case of electric vehicles, reducing weight and thus extending range.

Imagine a solar farm which has a choice between using inverter A weighing 2 tons or inverter B weighing 200 kg. Inverter B is a little more efficient, thus boosting annual yield by 1% or 2%, but otherwise all else in terms of reliability, life span, etc. is equal. You would go for the lighter inverter because, in doing so, you would avoid the need for a substantial concrete platform and the use of a crane; you'd be able instead to manually lay a few concrete paving slabs and maneuver the inverter into place with a hand-cranked pallet truck. This is just a small example of a modest strategic investment aimed at delivering more efficient and cost-effective solutions for solar and wind power as well as electric transportation.

*Google's Self Driving Car*

For a number of years, Google has been working on the development of self-driving cars, and recently unveiled a prototype without a steering wheel or pedals. This development proved controversial with California – one of several states authorizing the use of self-driving test vehicles, yet refusing to allow the vehicle to operate without the ability to take over manual control. (Earlier Google self-driving cars were modified production models which featured all the manual controls allowing a driver to take over if necessary.)

Clearly, the technology for self-driving cars has reached the point at which remaining barriers to public adoption are rapidly falling away, with possibly more political and legal than technical hurdles remaining. Already, some self-driving features are appearing on production cars – such as automatic reverse parking, and electronic braking assist which automatically applies the brakes to prevent a vehicle running into the vehicle in front. As time goes by, more such features will appear leading to self-driving production cars with manual override, and finally fully autonomous vehicles similar to the Google prototype described above.

This has the potential to provide numerous benefits to the environment:

-   Fewer cars on the road – A small fleet of autonomous cars can easily replace a larger fleet of private cars belonging to individuals. Using a phone app or similar, it will be possible to call a vehicle when needed. As at any given time, most cars are parked somewhere, there is clearly a substantial amount of unused transport capability at any given time. Autonomous vehicles would run for a far higher portion of the time, thus reducing the number of vehicles needed overall, cutting embodied emissions associated with vehicle manufacture as well as building and maintaining car parking facilities, and reducing congestion on the roads as the number of parked vehicles reduces.

-   The right vehicle for the job – Many owners have a vehicle which is far larger than required for their common daily needs, since they chose a vehicle capable of serving their most demanding requirements. With an autonomous vehicle, if one person is going across town to see a friend, a 1 or 2 seater micro-car is adequate, while if taking a 7-person family on a caravan holiday, a 4-wheel-drive 7-seater vehicle can be selected. That way, users do not take an extra ton of unnecessary metal with them everywhere they go when the larger vehicle is only needed for a few journeys a year.

- More efficient vehicles – As any given vehicle is on the roads far more, travelling greater annual distances per vehicle, the extra capital cost of more energy efficient technologies has a far stronger business case. The average efficiency of autonomous vehicles is therefore likely to be much higher.

- Electric vehicles – Fully autonomous vehicles will almost certainly be electric vehicles, most likely using induction charging. This will allow the vehicle to "refuel" itself, greatly reducing the need for human intervention to keep the vehicle on the road.

- Facilitating distributed generation – Smart charging of autonomous vehicles will allow solar or wind power to be more easily managed on the power grid, with charging most likely to occur when power is most easily available.

*Drone Delivery*

Another Google project is the development of delivery drones for local goods distribution, so that while bulk goods might be delivered to a city by truck or train, delivery of small items within the city to pick up points such as local shops could be achieved using small unmanned electric drones. This has the potential to greatly reduce delivery miles for traditional delivery vehicles. Such drones would fly directly between two points, avoiding the extra distance imposed by the geography of the road network and one-way traffic circulation, and have far lower emissions per delivery than occur when delivering packages to many different locations using a vehicle weighing several tons.

# Tesla

*Its Products*

Tesla is a rapidly expanding manufacturer of electric cars whose demand for batteries is already of such a size that it is creating a potential shortage in the market for lithium batteries. Tesla has already installed a large number of charging stations across the U.S. and elsewhere, many of which incorporate solar power generation. Tesla is currently in the process of developing a $5 billion lithium battery factory (in conjunction with Panasonic) which, on its own, will have more manufacturing capacity than all existing lithium battery facilities combined. In addition, rather than being satisfied with one such facility, Tesla appears intent on breaking ground on at least two other sites simultaneously, and apparently plans on building more such facilities as the requirement for such batteries in electric vehicles, and for off-grid solar expands.

*Its IP*

In a highly unusual move, Tesla recently threw open its entire patent portfolio to any person or company who in good faith wants to use the technology. While this may appear crazy to those with a traditional mentality, Tesla CEO Elon Musk apparently believes that doing so will free Tesla from having to expend resources defending its patents, help to drive innovation, assist in building the market for electric vehicle and battery technologies, and speed the learning curve for electric vehicles, making them competitive faster than would otherwise be the case. The company believes that this broad spectrum of effects will facilitate achievement of its business objectives.

Editorial note: I question the sanity of anyone who bets against Elon Musk.

## Apple Computer

Apple has been described as the most over-capitalized company in corporate history; it has a cash pile of $158.8 billion—more than three times the size of Google's. Apple is therefore in a financial position to fund very easily the introduction of whatever renewable energy resources it deems to have merit.

Like Google, Apple is now committed to powering all its stores, offices and data centers with 100% renewable energy (up from a present level of 73% as of 2013) and is offering free recycling of all its products.

Apple fully accounts for all its climate changing emissions and the lifetime emissions of all its products from manufacture, through use to final recycling and disposal. No other company goes as far to measure, verify and make reports at this level, and Apple is committed to a constant program of improvement in this regard.

Currently, the company has extensive renewable energy production on its own sites, and sources considerably more from local third party suppliers. In addition, e-books, films, music and software delivered on line require no physical manufacture, thus eliminating all the materials and physical distribution impacts of hard-copy books, etc.

Apple also has 300 EV charging points and 1000 shared bicycles on its campuses, promotes the use of public transport, and is building all its new facilities to the highest possible efficiency standards, some of which achieve LEED Platinum standard. In addition to its commitment to energy efficiency, Apple takes water efficiency seriously and is working to increase the re-use of water within its facilities, and to reduce overall water consumption.

All Apple products exceed Energy Star efficiency standards – with some tablets now 3.8 times as efficient and desktop 4.2 times as efficient as are needed to achieve Energy Star recognition. These products are also packaged in smaller and lighter containers, reducing the impact of transporting the goods from manufacturing facilities to customers.

Apple is also reported to be considering the acquisition of Tesla; talks (apparently) have already begun in this regard.

## Larry Ellison

Larry Ellison is one of the world's richest men; he bought the Hawaiian island of Lanai in 2012, and then set out to establish a demonstration two-way micro-grid based primarily on solar and wind power with compressed natural gas as back-up. The island also features wind powered desalination, and computer controlled drip-irrigated commercial crops. The system is designed to maximize water efficiency, using a variety of clever techniques; for example, should a part of a field be in shade, it receives less water than other areas which are in full sun.

While this project is said to be motivated more by environmental concern than profit, it is designed to demonstrate that green power and efficient water use can be cost-effective—obviously an extremely important point to be made.

## Bill and Melinda Gates

Bill Gates sees the energy industry as too large for philanthropic actions to have too great an impact. Thus he tends to stay away from mainstream renewable technology, and prefers to leave that to profit-motivated investors. However, he does see a role for strategic philanthropic involvement in early stage R&D into breakthrough energy technologies which he sees as vital to achieving a near-zero emission infrastructure.

The Bill and Melinda Gates Foundation has made a significant investment in Terra Power, a developer of 4th generation traveling wave nuclear reactors; the organization regards this as a possible breakthrough technology that might further its aim of clean energy.

Terra Power reactors are inherently safer than conventional nuclear plants, require far less uranium, give rise to far less high-level nuclear waste, and are expected to be far more cost-effective.

In addition, the foundation invests in renewable energy for off-grid clinics in the poorer parts of the world as an incidental part of meeting its philanthropic healthcare objectives.

# Ikea

The Swedish furniture giant Ikea is another company with an aggressive policy of investing in renewable energy; they currently boast a portfolio of 94 MW of solar and 345 MW of wind power. In 2013, Ikea produced 37% of its global energy requirements from renewable sources, and they have $2 billion allocated for further such investments through 2015. Their goal is to produce more renewable energy by 2020 than they are using.

In addition, Ikea has partnered with Hanergy, a Chinese solar energy giant, to sell solar arrays to domestic customers in the U.K. at a highly competitive cost.

Further, Ikea has a strong policy on energy efficiency; they eliminated incandescent lights from their product range ahead of any legal requirement to do so. In like manner, Ikea will stop sales of fluorescent lights by 2016, at which point they will only offer LED lamps.

On the social responsibility side, Ikea has developed solar-powered flat-pack refugee shelter units which are already being used by Syrian refugees in Lebanon. This took some negotiation with the Lebanese government, which feared that the well-built and relatively attractive shelters might encourage permanent settlement.

## Warren Buffett

Warren Buffet, CEO of Berkshire Hathaway, is widely considered the most successful investor of the 20th century. He is reported to be personally frugal despite enormous wealth, and has pledged to give away 99% of his $60+ billion fortune to philanthropic causes.

Among his investments are a $2 billion solar project and a 40% share in a $1.6 billion wind farm. In total Berkshire Hathaway has committed $15 billion to solar and wind power projects, and he has been quoted as saying that there's another $15 billion ready to go as far as he is concerned. The company is aided in this renewable energy expenditure by using the investment to offset profits in other parts of the business; the investment is quite effective from a tax perspective.

This is a good time to discuss taxation and its relationship to renewable energy. To that end, here is an excerpt from a Bloomberg article by Noah Buhayar and Jim Polson:

*Presently, any solar investment qualifies for a federal 30% investment tax credit set against taxable income. This applies all the way from small domestic solar arrays up to solar farms of hundreds of MW. In addition, some states and local administrations offer additional incentives in a variety of forms.*

*The Production Tax Credit for wind power expired in 2013 and then was restored for one year for projects starting construction before January 1, 2014.*

*There has been a history of on-off incentive policies which have undermined confidence and created uncertainty in the U.S. wind market, resulting in feast and famine years. For example, 2013 saw a very substantial reduction in new wind investment, with installations dropping from 12 GW in 2012 to 2 GW in 2013. (Investors rushed to complete projects in 2012 while the incentive was available, then avoided new projects in 2013 when they might not be completed in time to receive the incentive). 2014 is projected to be a stronger year of around 7 GW based on the extension of the production tax credit.*

*It should be noted that any on-off incentive arrangement is extremely bad policy repeatedly creating then destroying jobs and the motivation to invest. In the good years with incentive, everyone rushes to install as much as possible pushing up costs, then lets most of their staff go in the next period as there is insufficient work to justify their continuing employment. Far better to have a more modest but rock-solid policy framework with rules everyone can understand, with a structured approach to incentive changes based on evidence and agreed criteria. Any incentive to long-term planning and sustainable growth is destroyed by such incentive uncertainty.*

*For solar power, the tax credit remains in place until 2016, providing certainty for investments for the time being.*

*The present tax breaks are unlikely to continue in their present form; however, this is unlikely to make a large difference to the attractiveness of renewable energy investments in the medium- to long-term with both solar and wind power continuing to reduce their costs. Of the two, solar costs are declining faster from a higher base, and appear to have further to fall in the foreseeable future due to both opportunities to cut soft costs in markets like the U.S. and Japan, and due to technical factors like more efficient panels and lower panel and inverter costs per watt. Wind power is however already cost competitive in some locations with all other forms of generation even without the tax breaks.*

*With current projections for solar installed costs, especially if there is a concerted effort to reduce administrative soft costs, solar installations are likely to continue accelerating rapidly for as long as the investment tax credit remains in place with a particularly big year in the final year of the incentive. There is likely to be a dip in installations in the year after as many of that year's projects will be rushed forward to get the incentive. Following this one-year dip, the installation rate is likely once again to rise – this time on a pure market basis with costs having reduced sufficiently that a good return can be made without incentives.*

# Chapter Eleven—
# Electric Transportation Will Become Ubiquitous

I'm convinced of quite a few things with respect to electric transportation:

- The world is in the process of replacing petroleum distillates as fuel for transportation. We are finding that the numerous costs (extraction, shipping to remote refineries, military protection, terrorism, environmental damage, etc.) are becoming unacceptably large, and are getting worse.

- The world will soon focus on one or two alternate fuels; we will not evolve a great number of different approaches, e.g., hydrogen, CNG, propane, dimethyl ether (DME), etc., as the cost of scaling production and delivering all these different fuels is prohibitive.

- The ubiquity of electricity goes a long way to solving the problems associated with the delivery of this type of alternative fuel.

- Almost all large auto OEMs have made commitments in the direction of electric vehicles.

- A growing number of EVs are being charged with distributed generation, especially PV arrays.

- As more EVs are plugged into the grid, the more benefit they can provide in terms of absorbing off-peak power and providing ancillary services. Also, grid operators can use the flexibility by which EVs can be charged to integrate more renewables into the grid mix in their real-time decision making.

- All one billion cars and trucks on the world's roads can be replaced with a 14% increase in the generation of electrical power (due to the huge delta in efficiency associated with charging and discharging batteries vs. burning hydrocarbons).

- The presence of EVs and the implementation of smart grid are mutually re-enforcing.

Let's examine all this in some detail.

Electric transportation is ideally placed to play a major role in managing the variability of intermittent renewable power sources such as wind, solar, tidal, and wave power by providing grid-balancing services and enabling increased penetration of intermittent sources without adversely affecting grid stability.

For the moment, so as to preserve the life of vehicle batteries, it seems likely that this would take the form of "smart grid innovations" to manage charging in the best interests of grid stability.

Let's take an example: an electric vehicle owner parks in their workplace car park at 8:45 AM and plugs into their employer's vehicle charging point, knowing that the car will be needed at 5:00 PM, and would like to ensure that they have 80% charge at that time. The employee then uses a smartphone to instruct the charging point to top up their battery to a minimum of 80% state of charge before 5:00 PM. The employee does not care when during the day the battery gets charged, and leaves it to the grid operator to decide when and how fast to charge the car, and whether to continue charging the vehicle after it reaches 80% state of charge. The grid operator then slows down, speeds up, or interrupts charging as best suits grid stability.

For the moment, there are relatively few electric vehicles; however their numbers are growing fast, and as battery prices fall and vehicle range increases, adoption can only speed up.

## Position in Three to Five Years

Within a few years, there are likely to be millions of electric vehicles on America's roads, with a similar situation applying in the EU, Australia, China and Japan.

GM says that it intends to produce 500,000 pure electric cars annually by 2017, and many other, perhaps most, manufacturers are likely to have launched and begun ramping up production of their own electric vehicle models by that time.

Aggregated together, millions of vehicle batteries can appear to the grid as several gigawatts of "spinning reserve." E.g., if a 500 MW power plant suddenly cuts out when 1 GW of power is being fed into electric vehicles, the grid operator can instantly halve the amount of power going into the vehicles so as to offset the generation loss, giving time to adjust the output of other power plants. Conversely, if a weather condition runs through that rapidly ramps wind power generation by 1 GW, charging of the electric vehicles fleet can be sped up, and users who only require say 80% charge might return to their vehicles to find them fully charged.

# The Likely Longer-Term Position

By this time, a substantial proportion of new vehicles will be powered by electricity. Battery technology will have moved on enabling less costly, more powerful, lighter, more efficient and long lasting batteries to be supplied.

This opens the door to vehicles playing a substantially bigger part in managing the grid in various ways, over and above the currently feasible option to adjust the charging behavior of some vehicles according to the needs of the grid. Here are a few aspects of all this:

- Vehicle to grid – This is technically possible now, but tends not to be done due to the impact this might have on battery life. Batteries on the Tesla, Nissan Leaf and Chevy Volt (to name only the highest volume electric vehicle offerings) have batteries which will in many cases last as long as the vehicle, but would not easily stand up to regular use providing power to the grid during peak hours. In the near future, however, battery durability issues appear likely to be solved sufficiently such that every electric vehicle can both take power from the grid and deliver power back to the grid.

  In areas like Arizona and Hawaii for example, this will enable the installation of huge amounts of solar power generation with vehicles absorbing excess power generation during the day, and giving back some of this stored power during the evening demand peak as solar generation ends in the evening.

- Home UPS – With vehicle-to-grid technology comes the possibility of creating an islanded power supply for the home in the event of a power outage. Islanding is important, as it means isolating the house supply from the grid for the duration of the outage so that power delivered to the home cannot be exported, which would be a dangerous situation for utility workers when the supply is restored. This could be very useful in an emergency as an electric vehicle's fully charged battery can keep a home powered up for several days if lower priority electricity uses are curtailed.

- Essential services UPS – Assuming even minor improvements— and even with today's vehicles—it is possible to use electric vehicles to provide emergency power to essential services. For example, hospital staff with electric vehicles might be given free or discounted workplace vehicle charging in exchange for UPS services. In the event that the hospital is hit by a power outage, the electric vehicles at that time charging instead deliver power until backup generators can be started. Likewise, these vehicles and those of volunteers able to reach the hospital could provide this service during an extended outage when fuel might run low, such as might occur during very severe winter storms, during major flooding events, or earthquakes. It should be remembered that electric vehicles also include boats, which in an emergency, could potentially reach some places inaccessible by land vehicles.

- Off-grid homes – The Australian firm Star 8 Solar manufactures small solar-charged vehicles (that can also be plugged into the grid) called "TukTuks." Each TukTuk has two batteries, but can run on a single battery. At the end of the day, the TukTuk driver can remove one of the batteries from the vehicle to provide his family with light and phone charging. This vehicle has near zero costs of operation, and provides basic electrification; it's already having a significant social impact by reducing costs for drivers, and by enabling them to have a modest electrical supply at home in the evenings.

## Typical Vehicle Use

Typically vehicles stand idle for many more hours than they are traveling. In 2009, the average U.S. household had 1.86 vehicles, and used their own vehicles for 54.38 miles per day – an average of approximately 29 miles per vehicle per day. This implies that, on average, each vehicle is sitting idle for around 22 to 23 hours a day, a fact confirmed by other forms of research on the subject. Thus, for the most part, time of charging can be flexible, providing that sufficient charge is in the battery when the vehicle is needed.

## Other Likely Changes

As described above in the discussion on Google, the other major innovation now undergoing serious development is autonomous vehicles. For many urban dwellers in major conurbations, fully autonomous vehicles may well bring about the end of personal vehicle ownership. If you live in a large city with good public transport, owning a vehicle can be an expensive liability, with parking spaces often costing a small fortune, not to mention insurance costs and all the other expenses that come with owning a vehicle. In this situation, the obvious choice would be to call a "driverless cab" for the rare occasions when use of a private vehicle is essential, while sharing the costs with many other occasional users.

Of course, the electric vehicle is only one form of alternative fuel, but ultimately, it will prove to be the best. As mentioned above, competitive solutions include hydrogen fuel cells, as well as several different (and cleaner) hydrocarbons, e.g., natural gas, ethanol, propane, butanol, dimethyl ether, methanol, etc. At a minimum, the combustion of hydrocarbons releases $CO_2$ into the atmosphere, not to mention a certain level of other gases that damage the environment and human health.

Hydrogen fuels have the potential to operate with close to zero environmental impact. The issue is the way the hydrogen is derived; e.g., using solar energy to electrolyze water is a cleaner approach than reforming methane. There are two unavoidable issues with hydrogen, however. One is the efficiency of the process; even our best electrolyzers (which are quite expensive), suffer from efficiencies in the 60s. The other, and more important, is the fuel delivery infrastructure. In the U.S. alone, there are approximately 50,000 gas stations; retrofitting them for hydrogen would be a monumentally expensive task.

The delivery infrastructure for electricity, by contrast, is far more straightforward. Coincidentally, most gas stations are already equipped with 480 volt service, which can be used to charge EVs in a relatively short period of time, perhaps 20 – 30 minutes for a full charge. Further, as we've seen above, since most cars sit idle 23 hours per day in places that have electric service (home and at the workplace), creating this charging infrastructure is a relatively easy task.

## Environmental Impact

Of course, we need to ask ourselves the same question about electricity that we just posed about hydrogen, i.e., How is it generated? In particular, the question is: How do grid operators respond to an incremental load on the grid? Note that this is a much different question than: What is the average grid-mix? The answer to the second question is that, in the U.S., it was 39% coal in 2013, though this is irrelevant; we are not charging our cars with the average grid-mix. Since EVs represent an incremental load, only the first question comes into play, if we want an honest answer to environmental impact of electric transportation. And the answer to the first question, in the U.S., at least is that at night, when we are most prone to charge our cars, an incremental load is almost always met with coal, as that's the least cost form of baseload energy. Since coal is by far the dirtiest source of energy, we are forced to conclude that, at the present time, the environmental impact of EVs is dubious at best, and that this will only change when coal is not the go-to source of energy for grid operators.

Having said all this, for all the reasons I presented at the beginning of the chapter, including the fact that we're very close to being able to store off-peak wind cost-effectively, we're quite close to whacking coal as our chosen source for baseload at night. The moment that is the case, EVs will have a fabulous environmental impact.

## Other Externalities

Note that there are other externalities of oil that we tend to overlook. One of these is global hostility, aka, war.

The cost of operating the U.S. war machine is $640 billion per year, making it by far the largest military budget on Earth; in fact, we outspend the next 16 counties combined. The cost of the U.S. "presence" (to use a kind word) in Iraq and Afghanistan is estimated to exceed $4 trillion by the time (if any) we're finished there.

In addition to those dollars that could have been spent on health, education, the development of cleantech, or other programs to enhance the quality of life for all Americans, we need to acknowledge the cost in terms of dead and wounded soldiers. Somehow, we have put a dollar figure on a human life, I suppose for insurance purposes, though I'm not sure how Jesus or Socrates would view this mathematical exercise.

On top of that, we need to examine the fact that our much-discussed "addiction to oil" is empowering terrorists. Obviously, there is no way to put a cost on the mayhem done by terrorist groups around the world, but when we add up the damage associated with 9/11 in New York City, Bali, London, etc.—and factor in the effects of Isis in Syria and Iraq, Boko Haram in Nigeria, and the others, it's obviously a fantastically large number. Removing oil from the list of commodities that have value to humankind will act to dismantle the engine by which a great deal of this terrorism is powered.

# Chapter Twelve—
# Certain Concepts Are Clear Losers, Further Facilitating the Investment Decision-Making Process

This idea may seem to contradict the main theme of the book, but let's mull it over for a second. The energy challenge facing humankind is really simple: it's capturing the energy from renewable resources (mainly the sun) in the most efficient, least-cost manner possible and funneling it into three main areas: buildings (lighting and HVAC), industry, and transportation, the last of which is about 30% of the total; that's a big number.

Right off the bat we can see that this is bad news for things like biofuels. Let's take algae, which is clearly the best of all conceivable feedstocks, as it contains 30 – 50 times more energy per unit of mass than any terrestrial plant. However, building scalable plants to grow and process algae has proved to be an insurmountable challenge thus far, and there is very little reason for hope that the future will bring a change here.

This is essentially because of the basic thermodynamics associated with living organisms; they didn't evolve to store large quantities of energy they don't need for their metabolic processes. Organisms are built to survive and reproduce, not to store extra energy for us to put in our gas tanks. Even if I am wrong here, the progress of solar and wind, as discussed above, is happening at an incredible rate–more than fast enough to make the subject of algae (and thus all other biofuels) moot.

This is an example of using common sense and an extremely rudimentary understanding of science to see that certain overall concepts can't possibly succeed. And that's good news for investors in that it narrows the field. Isn't it easier to pick the winner in a horserace with five entrants than one in which there are 20? If biofuels are doomed to failure, that's good news for EVs and batteries, if only because it means that one more competitor has been eliminated.

To be fair, this isn't a completely black and white issue, and I'm not saying that all investors in biofuels are fools. Biofuels can play a role in delivering clean energy, at least for the next few decades, but that role will be limited, particularly in the light of increasing demands for food, water and arable land with which such cultivation is likely to compete, as climate disruption further threatens future food security.

There are, however, biomass resources which can be deployed for energy production with minimal adverse impacts such as the use of waste food, food by-products such as vegetable peelings, farm manure and sewage for the production of biogas via either anaerobic digestion or gasification technology. Anaerobic digestion also produces valuable fertilizer for the cultivation of next year's crops alongside energy, and removes weed seeds and pathogens. Solid biomass by-products such as straw and tree bark from forestry operations can also be deployed for energy purposes. As a general rule, solid biomass is probably best deployed for heat in the form of cooking fuel in the developing world, and space / industrial heat production in the developed world.

A modest production of liquid biofuels can also be achieved in a sustainable manner with that fuel possibly best deployed in the activities where few alternatives exist to liquid fuels. For example, it is hard to see how long-range air travel could be achieved as a commercial activity without the use of liquid fuels.

## Waste-to-Energy

Let's close this chapter by re-enforcing what I said here about waste-to-energy. In and around some of the world's largest cities is an enormous source of bio-energy in the form of municipal solid waste (MSW); Bangkok, Thailand, for instance, the world's 29th largest city, generates 14 thousand tons per day. This presents numerous problems in terms of land use and threats to human health. Using advanced technologies in thermal anaerobic gasification, we have the potential to get rid of all this waste and simultaneously generate significant amounts of power.

# Chapter Thirteen—
# Incentives To Lower Carbon Emissions Will Accelerate All This Even Faster

Each of the chapters above covers the migration to renewable energy on pure market-driven economics. Yet there are other pressures that will hasten the process, a few of which are covered here.

Of the over 200,000 groups on Earth whose purpose is social and environmental justice, arguably the most effective one focused on the migration away from fossil fuels is The Sierra Club, with its "Beyond Coal" campaign. The effort has three explicit goals:

- Retiring one-third of the more than 500 coal plants in the U.S. by 2020

- Replacing the majority of retired coal plants with clean energy solutions such as wind, solar, and geothermal

- Keeping coal in the ground in places like Appalachia and Wyoming's Powder River Basin

Beyond Coal has had an enormous impact on the sensibilities of the common American, bringing U.S. voters closer to Europeans in their thinking and behavior.

In addition, information and communications technology has been an enormous help in creating a social environment in which the horrific consequences of our fossil fuel addiction have begun to become well understood. Tools like Google Earth enable users to "fly" over West Virginia and surrounding areas, and see for themselves what mountaintop removal actually looks like. It's a sickening experience, but one that everyone should have.

In response to the growing concern among voters, government has begun to take a few important steps, summarized as follows:

# Cap and Trade – A Mechanism for Limiting Climate Change

### The History of Cap and Trade

The first implementation of cap and trade in the context of pollution abatement was put in place by the EPA in 1990. From the EPA website:

*"The Acid Rain Program was established under Title IV of the 1990 Clean Air Act Amendments to reduce acid rain and improve public health by dramatically reducing emissions of SO2 and NOx. Using a market-based cap and trade approach, the program sets a permanent cap on the total amount of SO2 that may be emitted by electric power plants nationwide. The cap is set at about one half of the amount of SO2 emitted in 1980, and*

*the trading component allows flexibility for sources to select the method of compliance. The program also sets NOx emission limitations for coal-fired units with some compliance flexibility, representing about a 27% reduction from 1990 levels."*

The mechanism was highly successful at curbing acid rain in the U.S., cutting $SO_2$ emissions from all regulated sources by 5.5 million tons per year between 1990 and 2002. This reduction was achieved for substantially less money than the original EPA cost estimate, and has resulted in a marked environmental improvement especially in the northeastern U.S., which had previously been badly affected by acid rain. This improvement in air quality is projected to result in health benefits worth $85 to $100 billion per annum by 2015; that's about 25 times the cost of the program.

## *CO2 Trading and The Kyoto Protocol*

*The Kyoto Protocol of 1997 proposed to implement a global cap and trade market for CO2 and other climate changing gases such as methane and chlorofluorocarbons. The agreement was supposed to bring binding obligations on developed world signatories to cap, and then reduce their national greenhouse gas emissions by set percentages relative to 1990 by 2012 while developing countries had no binding emission levels, but agreed to make voluntary efforts to curb their emissions. The protocol was turned into an international treaty in 2005 when the minimum 55 countries signed up, and originally was due to include the U.S. which initially signed, but then could not get the treaty ratified. (As it happened, the U.S. inadvertently and without ever ratifying the treaty ended up meeting its proposed 2012 target.) Canada ratified Kyoto but later withdrew in 2011.*

As a result of the agreement, a number of countries developed markets to trade greenhouse gas emission rights, the largest being the European Union Emissions Trading Scheme (ETS) run by the European Commission and started in 2005.

The ETS allows international trade in emissions (European Union Allowances or EUA) between EU countries, as well as a limited quantity of Certified Emission Reductions (CER) under joint implementation. CERs are obtained by projects in developing countries where implementation of emission reductions is achieved with the help of a partner in the EU. A limited proportion of CER certificates can be substituted for EUA certificates, allowing the agreed cap to be achieved at lower cost than by full implementation within the EU.

The Regional Greenhouse Gas Initiative includes California, 10 northeastern U.S. states, Norway, Switzerland, Japan, Alberta, New South Wales, and New Zealand. China has also launched pilot cap and trade markets in seven of its most populated cities and provinces with the aim of reducing emissions by between 15% and 19.5% relative to 2010.

# Criticisms of the Kyoto Protocol

The 37 industrialized countries which originally ratified Kyoto collectively exceeded their target by reducing emissions by an average of 16% by 2012; however some say that this was largely achieved through the collapse of the economies of the former eastern bloc countries, and by "exporting their emissions" to the developing world—particularly China—as much of the heavy energy intensive industry of the industrialized world relocated. On this basis, some question exists whether Kyoto achieved any overall global emission reduction, since Chinese production and the associated transport tend to be more emissions-intensive and less efficient than similar production in the developed world.

Also following the economic crisis of 2008, emissions in EU countries fell rapidly causing the price of EUAs to collapse and leading to a large excess of certificates in the EU market. While it would have been possible to accelerate emission reduction targets taking into account this drop in emissions, the EU failed to act decisively, and was unable to reach agreement for the withdrawal of an amount of EUAs sufficient to enable the market to drive ongoing emission reduction. Some have even sought to increase emissions so as to get the EU "back on track" to its original targets which have already been exceeded.

## Cap and Trade the Future

In the developed world, there is an increasing requirement for large companies to account for their $CO_2$ emissions, and to participate in a patchwork of local cap and trade markets. While it is possible that eventually a global market will emerge, for the moment, this complex and varying situation is likely to persist.

In the developing world, a number of countries are now committing to decrease the carbon intensity of their economies and reduce the growth in their emissions by 2020; this movement is led by China but also it involves India, Indonesia, Brazil and South Africa. China and South Korea are planning for National Emission Trading schemes.

According to Ernst and Young, businesses in all the major emitting and emerging countries will be carbon-constrained after 2020, with the prospect of national and regional markets linking up to form a global carbon market. For further information see Ernst and Young's report: "The Future of Global Carbon Markets."

The U.K., for example, has a number of different mechanisms for supporting renewables, and most EU markets have one or more mechanisms similar to those used by the U.K. Here's a short summary:

## Feed in tariff

For small scale renewables, the U.K. has a feed in tariff – this applies to solar, wind and hydro under 5 MW, anaerobic digestion under 500 kW, and very small CHP units up to 2 kW. The U.K. feed in tariff is a supplement payment paid for every kWh generated regardless of whether it's used on site or exported to the grid. The feed in tariff is inflation-adjusted and is paid for 20 years. In addition, exported power receives a 4.5p/kWh (approximately $0.07/kWh) export tariff. The feed in tariff rates are regularly adjusted (usually reduced) as the cost of renewable power systems change.

## Renewable Heat Incentive

A similar scheme applies to renewable heat. Heat from solar water heaters, biomass boilers, and heat pumps is eligible for payments similar to the feed in tariff, subject to certain conditions. There are two versions of the renewable heat incentive, one open to non-domestic users such as businesses and public buildings, and the other open to households.

## Energy Company Obligation

Under the energy company obligation, there is a small levy on energy bills which the energy companies use to fund energy saving measures giving priority to vulnerable households. The money from this levy is then used to fund home insulation.

## Green Deal

Under the Green Deal, homes and businesses are first provided with an energy audit through which options for cost effective energy saving / renewable energy solutions are identified, following which the home or business can apply for a loan secured on the premises and paid for during the loan period through the customer's electricity bill by savings arising from the improvement.

Measures which can be funded under the Green Deal include double glazing, solid wall insulation (for older buildings without cavities), biomass boilers, solar water heaters, etc.

In some cases, insulation will be paid for by a levy on the energy companies under the energy company obligation.

## Renewable Energy Obligation Certificates

Larger renewable energy projects are partly funded by Renewable Obligation Certificates (ROCs). Projects between 500 kW and 5 MW have a choice between FIT and ROC mechanisms while those above 5 MW are required to sign up to the ROC mechanism. Under this scheme, major electricity producers and large energy intensive businesses such as steel makers are required to source an increasing proportion of their electricity (adjusted annually) from renewable sources. Producers of renewable electricity earn ROCs for each MWh of electricity they generate. The exact amount of ROCs allocated varies with technology with solar farms, offshore wind, wave power and tidal current generators receiving more certificates than onshore wind, which is currently a lower cost technology in the U.K.

For example, an onshore wind farm will earn 0.9 ROCs per MWh. These certificates are then sold at prices set by the market to organizations which are required to obtain a proportion of their electricity from renewable sources. In addition, the wind farm will sell its electricity in the marketplace using either a power purchase agreement, or by selling electricity on the spot market.

Like the feed in tariff, the ROC scheme is subject to regular adjustments as eligible technologies mature. The ROC system is due to be phased out and replaced with a new support system known as "contracts for difference."

## Contracts for Difference

Under "contracts for difference," a supplier of renewable or nuclear electricity will sell their electricity into the market in the normal way, and receive a supplement called the "contract for difference," giving them a fixed selling price for the life of the contract, at a level somewhat above current market rates. If market prices rise, the supplement will get smaller, and may eventually become negative if market prices exceed the fixed price.

The rates set vary with different technologies, and will also be subject to regular reviews of set prices for new suppliers.

This of course does not preclude the producer's negotiating a merchant sale in the market and opting out of the support mechanism if they believe that future rises in market prices will give them a better return.

# Chapter Fourteen—
# More on Heightened
# Consumer Sensibilities

There is evidence that the public appears to have reached its "credulity limit." It's true that the fossil fuel industry spends a fortune to deliberately and aggressively misinform the people, but it's clear that the common U.S. voter is starting to question what he's being told about the validity of fossil fuels, climate change, ocean acidification, loss of biodiversity, lung disease, etc.

Further accelerating this process, there's also an excellent chance that "corporate personhood," i.e., the infamous "Citizens United" U.S. Supreme Court decision of 2010, will be overturned; several states have introduced legislation to this effect, and the movement enjoys enormous popular appeal from a variety of different political persuasions.

As mentioned in the previous chapter, the efforts of the more than 200,000 groups whose missions are environmental and social justice have turned the tide, and appear to be overwhelming the forces of "evil" (call it what you will: greed, selfishness, oppression, etc.) that exist in the fossil fuel industry. To take an example, Koch Industries is spending hundreds of millions of dollars annually to demonize clean energy, create doubt on the validity of climate change, sue several of the states that have renewable portfolio standards, and take a range of other legal action to block in the incursion of renewables. But where has this gotten them? With the possible exception of Monsanto, they're the most reviled—and most wisely disbelieved—corporation on the face of the planet.

On another front, patriotic Americans are beginning to see that it's critical that the U.S. embrace clean energy, largely for national security concerns. The world's addiction to fossil fuels does more to empower the enemies of democracy than any other single factor.

In addition to national security we should note that American economic leadership is also at stake here; if the U.S. is to avoid the unenviable position of losing its relevance in the global marketplace, it cannot pretend that the world's complete retooling of the energy industry does not exist. Each of the major countries of the world is running at this exciting new business arena at warp speed; the U.S. will most certainly lose its position of economic leadership if it continues along with its head in the sand.

*Some Countries Have No Choice in the Matter*

According to statesman Henry Kissinger, "Nothing clears the mind like lack of choice." Here, unfortunately, the U.S. isn't forced in the direction of clean energy, as we do have a choice. However, many other countries are indeed forced to go to renewables. Consider the difference between the U.S. and Germany, for instance. Germany has no natural gas to speak of, and must buy it from Russia, which, needless to say, is far from an ideal situation; thus the development of an alternative is rightfully an extremely high priority.

For better or worse, the U.S. has tons of natural gas, not to mention other fossil fuels. This creates a choice, and that is based on more than the mere existence of the commodities themselves; oil, coal and gas companies employ hundreds of thousands of people, and they rake in hundreds of billions of dollars that they use to twist and distort our law-making processes through lobbying; the oil companies retain more lobbyists than any other industry on the planet.

ExxonMobil could have paid for every dollar of campaign funding in this mid-term election with 3% of the $138 billion in profit (not revenues) it earned last year. Having said all this, it's hard to imagine Exxon's demanding that a Congressman it bought foster the development of fossil fuels when renewables are less expensive.

## Global Poverty

In much of the developing world, solar power can be a significant part of the answer, as the solar resource is good throughout the year, the power grid is relatively undeveloped, domestic electricity demand tends to be at a low level even when grid electricity is available, and connection to the grid is affordable only to the rich. It should be noted that for families in communities which have not previously had any access to electricity other than by paying to have their mobile phones charged, access to even 10 or 20 Watt-hours per family per day combined with LED lighting and the ability to charge phones and other small devices at home can bring about a hugely positive social impact. This carries with it the capacity to provide educational opportunities, cut living expenses substantially, offer opportunities to increase productive activity, reduce lung disease arising from kerosine fumes, and enable safer management of important life events such as childbirth.

## New Sensibilities Become New Laws That Will Drive This Process

There are numerous areas in which new legislation will encourage the rapid installation of rooftop solar and other technologies to lower the overall eco-footprint associated with residential, commercial, and industrial real estate. In most cases, these laws already exist outside the U.S., serving as models that guide our thinking here in America.

Here are a few concepts that seem to be headed for law:

- Making an energy audit a requirement for selling or renting out a home. (This has been a legal requirement across the European Union since 2009, and it seems to be finally headed in the direction of the U.S.)

  My colleague Dr. Tom Konrad writes about movements towards voluntary energy audits: "These voluntary moves are a start, but making energy use disclosure mandatory, as opposed to voluntary, should help bring along the reluctant majority who are not already following these practices. If an energy audit or past energy bills were required to be provided by the seller or landlord whenever a building is sold or leased, buyers and renters could decide for themselves how much more they would be willing to pay for an efficient building, and the current owner would have an incentive to make cost-effective improvements beforehand." He most certainly has a point here.

  The city of Austin, the capital of Texas, recently passed an Energy Conservation Audit and Disclosure (ECAD) ordinance, Austin City Code Chapter 6-7, which requires that before the sale of their home, owners of residential buildings must have an energy audit performed, and that they *must* provide the results to prospective buyers.

- Additions to the building codes, e.g., requiring that new buildings would have to include the lesser of a) enough solar to supply a certain percentage of expected electricity use, or b) as much as is feasible given the solar access of the site.

- Reducing the time, hassle, and expense of permitting small solar PV projects. Anything under 3.6 kilowatts in the U.K. requires no permit at all.

# Part Three:
## Important Clean Energy Investment Opportunities Are Here and Now

Searching for clean energy technology is challenging: inventors want money to fund theories when their science is questionable… a certain prototype "works," (i.e., generates energy, but clearly won't scale to do so cost-effectively…an idea looks promising, but not in the face of a competitive approach that appears even stronger. Add on top of that the obvious: the couple of trillion dollars of private capital that is sitting on the sidelines, if it comes on the field at all, is much more likely to be aimed at building the next Google or FaceBook than getting into something that is capital intensive.

However….

After reviewing literally thousands of ideas for clean energy businesses over the past few years, here I present a brief summary of a few of my favorites that have the potential to provide transformative results in the cleantech arena. Are they right for all angel investors, VCs, family offices, and private equity firms? No. Are they right for a few? Absolutely.

I hope readers will find this section interesting.

# Wind Farm in the Southern U.S., Will Implement Compressed Air Energy Storage

Over the past few years, I've come to know a certain top-flight engineering team whose goal is to offer large quantities of baseload power from wind. Of course, the very notion requires energy storage, as wind is a variable resource. Here is a brief outline on the subject:

> Wind/CAES has far greater value than wind-only. Wind energy generated at night or during possible grid curtailment is stored as compressed air in natural, cavernous, geologic formations such as depleted natural gas wells. During the day, if the wind isn't blowing, compressed air is released and run through combustion turbines to create electricity. $H_2$ from electrolysis replaces natural gas used in existing CAES plants to heat stored air, making the power production system completely renewable.
>
> CAES solves problems, e.g., grid problems caused by intermittent wind, risk of curtailment issues, and dispatchability (less than 10 minutes). The subject isn't new, it just hasn't been developed. Though there are only two plants that have been deployed internationally, their stories are impressive:
>
> Huntorf, Germany - 290 MW CAES plant
>
> Operating successfully since 1978
>
> 31 years of outstanding performance
>
> 95% running reliability
>
> McIntosh, Alabama - 110 MW CAES plant
>
> Operating successfully since 1991
>
> 18 years of outstanding performance

81% operating efficiency kW in/kW out

97% running reliability

All sites proposed by this company provide Class 4 + winds and ideal access to CAES geologic formations. Texas & Kansas are ranked #1 & #2 in wind resource potential in the United States.

All sites provide access to wastewater resources needed to make $H_2$ from electrolysis, and have transmission lines planned or under construction.

*Research on High Voltage Transmission Suggests Rapid Deployment*

- Princeton Environmental Institute Report on CAES, by Samir Succar
- National Renewable Energy Laboratory Study, by Paul Denholm supports Wind/CAES
- Electricity Advisory Council & Electric Power Research Institute Study on Energy Storage
- The Ridge Energy report on Wind/CAES

*Excellent Regulatory Support*

- American Recovery and Reinvestment Act supports new energy technology including Wind/CAES
- Federal Energy Regulatory Commission support for building transmission lines in the Midwest (EIPC), SPP highway/biway
- Kansas legislature passes the first bill in history supporting CAES development; California has passed a similar bill supporting CAES and Texas has one on the docket
- Investment Tax Credits for wind projects can be traded for CASH with the Treasury Department

- ERCOT, MISO, and PJM are developing ancillary services pricing standards. Other RTO's are planning this as well.
- Waxman Markey bill for Cap and Trade of $CO_2$ is an incentive to develop Wind/CAES
- States' RPS will increase demand for wind power by 250% by 2015.

# Thermal Anaerobic Gasification: Unique, Patented Approach

Thermal Anaerobic Gasification is a thermochemical process that, while adding little or no atmospheric oxygen, changes the form of the feedstock, releasing energy that can be harnessed for use.

Most forms of gasification of certain types of feedstock, like treated lumber, e.g., railroad ties, result in carcinogens like dioxin, one of the most toxic chemicals on Earth. This is a unique, patented approach that cleverly works around this issue, and, more generally, offers ten positive operational points when compared to other available systems and process designs. In particular, the system/technology:

1. Is one of the only near oxygen-free continuous material feed systems / process designs able to limit CO2 production.
2. Does not make use of large amounts of water within the process design. Water usage within these systems is low, with most water usage reclaimed and reused.
3. Operates at reasonably low temperatures which allows for energy savings.
4. Has the ability to recover water/ moister out of the first phase of the system, allowing for the creation of a dry gas which can be utilized without the introduction of a damaging catalyst.
5. Is computer controlled and easily operated.
6. Is a modular design system that can be expanded as needed at a certain site, or set up in a decentralized format, able to process from 10 tons to 1,100 tons a day within one line.
7. Because of its modularity, enables a plant to be constructed off-site and shipped to the site easily, thereby cutting construction timelines.
8. Is on par lower than other technologies in terms of cost.
9. Can feed & process a wide range of feed materials including:

## Waste from Oil Refineries;

-- Spent catalyst contaminated with hydrocarbons and recovery of the metals
-- Tank bottoms
-- Soil contaminated with oil or other hydrocarbons
-- Contaminated towels, rugs, papers, etc.
-- All types of organic hazardous, toxic and non-hazardous waste

## Waste from chemical plants;

-- Ml types of organic chemical compounds including hazardous and non-hazardous waste
-- PCB contaminated oils, soil and any other matrix
-- Waste streams contaminated with dioxins
-- Waste water treatment sludges
-- Soil remediation
-- Activated carbon remediation

## Metallurgical Industries;

-- Rolling mill waste
-- Hazardous and non-hazardous sludges.
-- Soil remediation

## Electronic Waste;

-- Spent pastes and recovery of metals (hazardous waste)
-- Plastic and chlorinated plastics
-- Organic hazardous and non-hazardous waste

## Mining Industries Waste;

-- Soil remediation
-- Waste stream after leaching or amalgamation
-- Destruction of hazardous and complex chemical compounds

## Waste from Municipalities

-- Used tires with recovery of Carbon Black and steel as by-products
-- Municipal solid waste
-- All types of plastics, including chlorinate

10. Is a low-maintenance long-life cycle system and has a predicted operation year effectiveness of 94.5%.

# Modular Pyrolysis Technology: Perfect for Waste-Tire-to-Fuels/Electricity

300 million scrap tires are land-filled each year in the U.S. alone, a terrible waste of chemical energy and other valuable components. People have been talking about this subject for decades, attempting to create some sort of gasification/pyrolysis technology to this feedstock, though most have been fraught with technology issues. These people have "cracked the code" with technology that is working 24/7 without a glitch.

# Biogas/Biofertilizer Plant in Southern Pakistan

The manure from 400,000 buffaloes in a tightly confined area of Southern Pakistan is creating one of the worst ecological disasters and threats to human health on the planet. A talented team of people stands ready to expand their pilot plant that is creating small but predictable amounts of compost, liquid fertilizer and biogas up to the scale necessary to tackle the problem, while creating an income stream of over $100 million annually.

Landhi, a suburb of Karachi, is home to 400,000 buffalo that provide virtually all the milk and meat for the city's 20+ million residents. The animals are confined to a few square kilometers, and produce over 8,000 tons of dung ... each day. The subject company will use that manure to produce over 800,000 tons of compost annually, and, from the revenues they derive, will build and operate the largest animal biogas plant in the world.

## Synthetic Fuels

Some argue, quite convincingly, that, whether we like it or not, liquid fuels will be around for a very long time. The CEO and CTO of this team, a Ph.D. in physics, has developed a series of processes that take the off-peak wind energy, which totals about 25 terawatt-hours annually in the U.S. alone, and uses it to drive a series of chemical processes, resulting in high-grade diesel and gasoline. For those looking for the ultimate home-run, this could be attractive, since, if it happens, it's going to happen big.

Here's a brief description of the concept, whose inventor has dubbed: **WindFuels™**.

What are WindFuels™? The concept is really not complicated. We will use energy generated by wind to power processes that will recycle waste carbon dioxide into transportation fuels for automobiles, like diesel, ethanol or gasoline. We can also make fuels like jet fuel and propane. (We are talking mostly about fuels, but the FTS process can also produce ethylene and propylene which are used to make plastics – used in everything from textiles to tables.)

We'll **recycle** $CO_2$ from power plants or other exhausts (which release $CO_2$ into the air, contributing to global warming). Because we have removed the $CO_2$ from the air to make the fuels, using (burning) WindFuels releases no new carbon, making it a carbon neutral process. Replacing oil with WindFuels will reduce total $CO_2$ emissions by 40%.

No experienced chemist doubts that it is possible to convert $CO_2$ to fuels. The problem has been that prior proposals for doing this conversion have had efficiencies of only 20% to 30%.

The combination of the eight major technical advances we have made over the past five years will now permit this conversion to be done at 60% efficiency. That's high enough for carbon-neutral fuels made from waste $CO_2$ that will easily compete with petroleum on a cost basis, especially when the input energy is from excess wind energy in the middle of the night.

What we are doing is not magic. It is just good chemistry, physics, and engineering. Because we are using the carbon from waste $CO_2$ rather than coal, we have to add a lot of energy from wind. However, when all the processes are properly optimized, the cost of this energy becomes affordable. It is a small price to pay to dramatically reduce greenhouse gases in the atmosphere and provide a limitless supply of clean transportation fuels.

Fuels like ethanol, gasoline and jet fuel are hydrocarbon fuels. Hydrocarbons and alcohols are chemicals that contain hydrogen (H), carbon (C), and oxygen (O). We will use water ($H_2O$) and the waste (polluting) carbon dioxide ($CO_2$) from power-plant smokestacks to provide the carbon, oxygen, and hydrogen needed to make fuels like ethanol ($C_2H_5OH$) and gasoline ($C_8H_{18}$).

# Collection of Run-of-River Hydro Projects in Southern Brazil

Here's a description, beginning with an overview of the energy markets in the country generally.

*Foreign Investment in Brazilian Energy*

Private, foreign investment in the electricity sector in Brazil is both an old and very recent phenomenon. From the earliest hydroelectric projects in Sao Paulo and Rio de Janeiro in the late 1800s (built to power public transportation in those two cities) and small facilities in remote locations to power the mining and weaving industries, foreign investors were at the forefront of electric power in Brazil during the first half of the 20th Century.

Most foreign ownership was nationalized in the 1960s and all development, construction and distribution of the electricity was done by large state and federal companies from the 60's through the middle of the 1990's. Throughout this time, hydroelectric production dominated in Brazil; almost 80% of electric power was generated by hydro into the 1990s.

Privatization began about 1994 under the administration of Henrique Cardoso. A severe shortage of power and consequent rationing (2001-02) led to the opening of the "small" hydro market (< 30 MW) to private development and the overhaul of regulations in 2004. Among the changes made at that time was the right to enter into private PPAs with large users (of which Brazil has many), the streamlining of the approval and permitting of small hydro ("PCH"), and numerous reductions in cost and taxes for these products.

There was a rash of entry into this segment after the adoption of these new regulations, but often by groups that lacked the expertise and financial resources to finalize the licensing process, or ultimately to construct the project. Consequently, during the last five years, the segment has been undergoing a consolidation. There are, however, many opportunities resulting from this dynamic.

*Increasing Demand for Energy*

Brazil continues to be "behind the curve" in the approval and construction of new power production capacity. While the economy has been "flat" for much of the last three years, electric power consumption continues to grow at an annual rate of over 5%, fueled mostly by increased consumer consumption from a rapidly expanding middle class; over 30 million Brazilians have entered the middle class in the last 15 years.

More recently, wind power generation has begun to play a role and it is anticipated that solar will gradually gain traction in Brazil's renewable matrix but it is hydro that still dominates the market and there are many small (PCH) opportunities remaining in the south and southeast of the country where 70% of the population and demand is located.

## 25° Capital Ltda.

25° Capital Ltda. is a Brazilian company (majority owned by American shareholders) that specializes in corporate and project administration in the real estate and energy sectors in Brazil. Located in Curitiba (the capital of the State of Parana), the company has acquired numerous large, well located urban tracts over the last seven years and has contracted with key figures in the electric energy segment to provide opportunities for creating a "pipeline" of projects (greenfield to shovel ready) for companies looking to invest mid- to long-term in the Brazilian renewable electric market.

IRRs in good projects in the market can comfortably yield returns in the 14% – 16% range.

# Ocean Thermal Energy Conversion

I happen to be a shareholder in a smallish but rapid-growth company that dominates the world of ocean thermal energy conversion (normally abbreviated "OTEC"), a technology that extracts the heat from the warm waters near the surface of the world's tropical seas. The company, OTECorporation, leads this industry that will soon deliver clean baseload electricity to a great many of the more than one billion people who live within 1000 miles or so of the equator.

Here's a short exposition on the company, the technology, and, most importantly, the incredible business potential associated with all this.

*The Technologies: OTEC & SWAC*

80% of the sun's solar energy is stored in the surface waters of the world's oceans, and OTEC taps into that vast renewable energy resource by using the temperature differential between the warm surface water and cold deep ocean water to make clean baseload (24/7) electricity.

In 2009, after more than 30 years and $300 million spent on OTEC R&D by the U.S. Department of Energy, the National Oceanic and Atmospheric Administration issued a report concluding that, using a single cold water pipe, a 10MW OTEC plant can now be built and successfully operated using all off-the-shelf components. With 20 years of rising oil prices, OTEC is now price-competitive in specific markets, such as tropical and subtropical locations paying exorbitant electricity prices ($0.30-$0.70/kWh) based on some of the dirtiest forms of fossil fuels imported from great distances.

Unlike intermittent renewable energy sources such as wind and solar, OTEC provides reliable 24/7 electricity. And even relatively small OTEC facilities can drive desalination plants that produce large quantities of potable water. For example, the company's designs for one OTEC plant on a U.S. Naval Base (approved by the Office of Naval Research) will use just 4 megawatts of the gross electricity output to produce 1.25 million gallons of potable water each day.

Closely related to OTEC, Seawater Air Conditioning (SWAC) utilizes the deep cold ocean water for cooling buildings, reducing electricity consumption by up to 90% compared to conventional systems. Both of these well-proven technologies can also help produce plentiful amounts of fresh drinking water, dramatically reduce carbon emissions, and potentially save customers millions of dollars in energy costs in appropriate markets. With 20 years of rising oil prices, OTEC is becoming profitable while SWAC is already commercialized and successfully operating in several locations around the world.

*Ocean Thermal Energy Corporation (OTE)*

Headquartered in Lancaster, Pennsylvania, USA, and with offices or operations in Virginia, USA; Hawaii, USA; London, UK; Nassau, The Bahamas; US Virgin Islands and The Cayman Islands, OTE is first-to-market with the largest deep ocean hydrothermal project in the world, providing clean energy-saving air conditioning for the $3.5 billion Baha Mar luxury resort, scheduled to open in the first half of 2015.

OTE has generated a robust pipeline of global customers and projects for OTEC and SWAC plants, each with projected gross revenues to OTE of $400 million - $900 million.

Both technologies can also yield significant supplemental revenue streams by providing the valuable nutrient-rich deep ocean water resources for voluminous fresh drinking water through desalination and opportunities for sustainable fish-farming and agricultural enhancement projects.

OTE's mission is to meet the large global demand for its technologies, bringing environmental, social, and economic benefits to millions of people worldwide.

*Global Market*

According to the U.S. Department of Energy's National Renewable Energy Laboratory (NREL), there are more than 100 countries and territories on Earth with conditions appearing favorable for OTEC and SWAC facilities. And with many of these locations having numerous sites for these clean technologies, there are literally hundreds of potential OTEC and SWAC applications in the tropics (home to over one billion people and even the subtropics (home to an additional two billion). Ocean Thermal Energy Corporation is serving as the developer to build, own and operate OTEC and SWAC systems globally, serving this vast international market.

*Public Listing*

OTE is a recently listed public company with stock listing at about US$1.15, reflecting an increase in share price of approximately 35% compared to the opening price of US$0.85.

OTE has filed a Regulation A Offering Statement with the SEC. When approved it will allow OTE to raise an additional $5 million in a 12-month period. Shares sold pursuant to this offering are planned for sale at a price of US$1.50 per share, and will be free trading.

The company plans a 2015 up-listing to the main U.S. NASDAQ Exchange.

As a part of being a public company, OTE has received an independent analyst's research report on the Company, which concludes as follows: "The Company is a leading developer of SWAC systems and (to our knowledge) the only commercial developer of OTEC systems. The Company has a sound market penetration plan, has made significant progress to date, and is operating in an extremely large potential market – one that could eventually support as many as 500 10MW OTEC plants and several hundred SWAC plants. Furthermore, the Company has assembled a world-class leadership and engineering team that we believe are likely to succeed. Therefore, we initiate coverage of OTE Corp. with a Strong Buy rating, and set our 12-month price target at $2.00 per share."

# Converting Toxic Waste Streams Into High-Quality Building Products

This company maintains a proven, proprietary process by which it takes waste streams (some of them toxic, e.g., coal ash) and turns them into profit centers in the form of polymer composites, extruded into high-quality building products (especially roofing shingles) that are structurally superior in strength and stiffness, as well as resistant to fire, weather, mold and termites.

This unique and cost-effective process involves taking solid wastes (coal ash, mine tailings, waste glass, red mud, and incinerator ash) in dry granular form, mixing them with a liquid thermosetting polymer resin, and producing synthetic lumber goods. The procedure takes about a minute, and the products are ready to ship in an hour.

The business environment for this couldn't be stronger, in that there is no direct competition, and there is most definitely a growing concern about the toxicity of some of these waste streams, as well as a huge boom in sustainable building products of all types. Here's a brief outline:

*At a Glance*

- Waste streams turned into profit centers for green markets
- Proprietary, patented, highly-filled polymer composites
- A process that is fully developed and commercial
- Products are successful, green, and well-received
- Near 30% net profits

*Technology*

- Takes 65-75% solid wastes (coal ash, granite, mine tailings, waste glass, red mud, incinerator ash, and sand) in dry granular form,
- Mixes it with a liquid thermosetting polymer resin in an extruder

- Produces synthetic lumber and other composite products in about a minute. Ready to ship in an hour

*What's Special About the Technology?*

- Entry into many multi-billion dollar global markets
- No direct competition
- Very low product cost, due to foaming and cheap fillers - usually waste
- Low capital investment that can yield high sales volumes, with high ROI
- Very competitive thermoset building products that can compete in many markets - superior benefits

*Product Benefits*

- Structural, superior strength & stiffness
- Versatility to make virtually any building product, with any shape, any finish
- High durability & low maintenance
- Fire resistant, lumber has Class A fire resistance
- 150F heat resistant—thermosets don't soften with heat
- Mold & pest resistant
- No color variation; easily mass-colored or coated
- Workability: can use nails, screws, adhesive
- Weight - the density is adjustable: very light or very dense

*Why Are the Products So Valuable?*

- "Green" – have neutralized huge volumes of toxic chemicals
- Products survive what other products don't: fire, water, heat, termites, sunlight
- Consistent properties - filler variation doesn't alter the process

- Low cost materials and equipment - high margins

# Building Integrated Solar Thermal Hot Water Heating

Integrating solar energy of one form or another into building products is nothing new; however, this concept called "PlexiSun" is the very best out of many dozens I've come across over the years. The company has an internationally patented approach to providing hot water for residences of all types, and, more importantly, commercial and industrial buildings.

Imagine a dairy barn (where enormous quantities of hot water are needed), whose roof is constructed of a material that is capturing an impressive percentage of the sun's incident radiation and storing that energy for use.

PlexiSun is a solar thermal collector that is integrated into functional structures. It's constructed out of specially designed extrusions, using acrylic sheets that have been developed specifically for the construction industry, built in solar reflection surfaces.

The concept has a continuous flow system, and can be used to heat potable water supplies, or glycol for heating systems in frost zones. The modular design means the volume of heated fluid can be whatever is required; large volumes can be achieved as desired.

The prototype of this technology won the 2007 Supreme Award in the PSP Design Challenge, recognizing design and innovation. More recently, PlexiSun received very positive test results of a prototype application of its concept conducted at the TUV facility at Cologne, Germany, and a similar application of the PlexiSun concept is currently prototyped and being tested in Europe by a multi-billion-dollar German manufacturer.

# Part Four:

Short Essays on CleanTech and Sustainability, Originally Published as Part of the Blog at 2GreenEnergy.com

# Tactical Solutions Needed to Deal with Climate Disruption

United States Secretary of State John Kerry said recently that the U.S. is considering making a major contribution to a fund that would help developing countries deal with both the causes and the effects of climate disruption. Money would go to developing methods of reducing greenhouse gas emissions, and improving methods of handling droughts and floods.

This sounds good in principle, but, obviously, the fund is subject to mismanagement—even if all intentions are good and corruption is entirely absent. If I were directing this effort, I would take a very tactical approach, targeting a large number of small villages in many regions of the third world with a very simple toolkit:

- Microgrids based on distributed generation and storage, e.g., solar PV and batteries. (In places that have adequate feedstock, I'd substitute waste-to-energy systems.)

- Highly efficient lighting and computing for homes and schools, and refrigeration for medical clinics.

- Aeroponics, a highly cost-effective approach to sustainable agriculture that minimizes the consumption of water and other resources associated with growing large quantities of produce.

There are numerous benefits of this "one-size-fits-all" line of attack, and they fall into two groups. In the first group are all the ways in which this approach is highly efficient, i.e., reasons that a very large percentage of money is made available to address the problem. Minimizing the complexity of the solution greatly reduces the amount of administration required for decision-making, purchasing, executing on logistics, training, installation, and maintenance. It also removes a great deal of the potential for pork-barrel spending on items of dubious value. Simultaneously, it maximizes the pace with which we move through the learning curve and develop economies of scale.

In the second group are the numerous social benefits, as the effort "kills many birds with one stone":

- Reducing deforestation by providing a clean alternative source of energy.

- Removing toxic fumes from the burning of kerosene lamps and improving health generally.

- Improving education, thus raising human productivity and prosperity, while reducing women's fertility in the places with the highest rates of population growth.

If Mr. Kerry wants to look me up and invite me to participate, I'm not that hard to find.

# Here's Why Chevron Couldn't Make Biofuels Work

According to an article in Renewable Energy World, "Chevron Corp.'s attempts to turn plants into alternative fuels for profitable, large-scale production have failed." The author goes on to note:

*The second-largest U.S. oil company by market value spent "significant sums" and assigned some of its best scientists to evaluate more than 100 kinds of feedstock and 50 techniques for converting them into fuels without success, Chevron Chairman and Chief Executive Officer John Watson said during an address to the Economic Club of Minnesota in Minneapolis today, "The smartest minds in my company and others haven't yet cracked the code on pairing the right feedstock conversion technology and logistics in an economic and scalable package," Watson said.*

Maybe this is true because the concept is essentially folly in the first place. Not a single species evolved so as to retain more chemical energy than it needs to live, grow, and reproduce. Given that, the reason Chevron couldn't find a plant that would serve as a workable feedstock for us to power our one billion cars and trucks is not all that hard to guess: none exists. The process of evolution worked very hard over the past four billion years to ensure precisely that.

Now that we have that behind us, let's see where Chevron goes. If they're people of integrity, there is only one path they can possibly take (after they repair the damage they caused in Ecuador), and that is getting on board solving the world's energy problems in a realistic way. Here's a hint: look up. Our Earth receives 6000 times more power from the sun than all of humankind is consuming. We need a solution, or a set of solutions, that harvests 1/6000th of that power.

It's a challenge we can—and will—surmount. If Chevron wants to help, that's all good.

# PBS's "Ask This Old House" Recommends Energy Efficiency – But Misses the #1 Reason To Care About It

I like to watch the PBS show "Ask This Old House" on Saturday mornings. I'm so impressed with the incredible level of professionalism and the cleverness of the solutions these folks come up with.

Whenever it's possible to mention energy efficiency or solar energy, the plumbing and heating guy, Richard Trethewey, normally dives right in. He does a great job explaining solar thermal hot water heating, solar photovoltaics, and all manner of solutions that reduce the waste of energy. But I'm amused that the show is very careful not to imply that there are ethical implications here, only that homeowners can reduce their electricity bills. Is environmentalism some sort of taboo subject?

It's sad that we feel inhibited about coming out and saying: "Hey, fellow Earthlings: we have a problem here. Our approach to using energy is not sustainable. It's ruining our planet, and we all share a collective responsibility to do something about it." Is being aware of the decay of our environment and having a conscience really such a dangerous thing to admit? "Ask This Old House" treats this as if they were gay people coming out of the closet in the 1950s, an era in which very few people made the admission, and those few did so at their peril.

Here's a note to Richard and the show's producers: It's actually a good thing to care about the world around you, and it's totally OK to admit it.

# Our Path to Sustainability

After I published my third book, *Renewable Energy – Following the Money,* in 2013, I took a break from efforts like this, as, frankly, I had run out of ideas. But just last week I twigged on something that I believe needs to be said, which I summarize here:

Most people who study the big issues facing our civilization believe that we're teetering on the edge of destruction. Yes, there are many different individual threats, e.g., climate change, but all this is complicated by the fact that these threats really can't be understood as "individual"; they interact with one another in ways that no one can accurately predict. For instance, runaway climate change and the resultant loss of farmland from sea level rise, salt incursion, and severe droughts might team up with ocean acidification and loss of biodiversity to cause food and water shortages, which will promote hostility among nations over the remaining scarce resources. Is this scenario likely? Sadly, yes it is. Is it the only one that's at all likely? Unfortunately, no.

But regardless of how these threats blend together, how many overall "scenarios" exist, how probable each one is, and how we measure all this, it's increasingly clear that this is a game that our civilization cannot afford to lose. Failure is not an option, if you'll pardon the cliché.

And, in truth, there are many reasons to believe that our society will, in fact, pull all of its ever-expanding list of human and technological resources together before it's too late. Indeed, this is a book of hope, of encouragement. It's a book that acknowledges that:

- anthropogenic climate change and numerous other environmental threats are quite real – and encroaching on us by the day......while pointing to a variety of pragmatic solutions

- there are "bad guys," e.g., powerful and greedy people and groups.......while explaining how these forces of selfishness may be in the process of losing the battle against the 200,000+ groups on Earth whose missions are environmental and social justice

- world economies face tough challenges and the middle class continues to shrink.......while examining the role of the clean-tech industry as a dynamic and empowering change-agent in the 21st Century

The purpose of the project is to examine the idea that the world is full of thoughtful and decent people who are behaving rationally in the face of crisis, and that, correspondingly, our civilization has an excellent chance of avoiding the disasters that are speeding its way.

# The Renewable Energy Industry Is All About JOBS

A political campaign ad from the woman who ran against Mitch McConnell for a U.S. Senate seat in Kentucky reminds me of an important issue—perhaps *the only* important issue—driving the ultimate success of the renewable energy industry in this country: the promise of *jobs*.

The ad depicts an out-of-work coal miner from Eastern Kentucky, providing Ms. Grimes the opportunity to promise how she'll put this fellow and thousands like him back to work. Never mind that he works in what is arguably the world's deadliest (legal) profession; the quality of the work isn't really the point here, rather, that the fossil fuel industry claims to be all about jobs.

They hope you won't look into this too closely and come to understand that there are 6.5 million jobs supported by renewable energy worldwide. That's not a promise, by the way; it's 6.5 million weekly paychecks. They hope you don't know that EnergyFactCheck.org hosts literally hundreds of articles that describe the huge profusion of jobs opening up every day in the U.S., as solar, wind and the rest continue to expand.

The fossil fuel boys are, of course, the wealthiest and most powerful industry in the history of humankind, and so it's to be expected that they are going to continue to spend some of that lucre to convince you that oil, coal and gas are the only games in town. But ask yourself: why are we hearing about this so much all of a sudden?

My guess is that, for the first time, they're threatened–and it's serious. 10 years ago, the fossil industry wasn't spending a nickel denigrating renewables; they didn't need to, as clean energy was barely a rounding error. Now, these folks are gazing in horror at some of the most critical facts—data points that become more alarming each week:

- Wind energy is close to five percent of the U.S. grid mix

- The cost of clean energy continues to plummet, and the efficiencies are rising

- Virtually every country other than the U.S. is taking seriously its responsibilities to migrate away from fossil fuels, based on concerns about climate change, ocean acidification, loss of biodiversity, lung disease, etc. How long can they continue to count on the ignorance of the American people?

The handwriting's on the wall. So what to do?

Attack, of course.

But the renewable energy industry's response isn't a counter-attack per se; it's not hysteria and lies; it's facts and reason; it's the truth about what is clearly destined to be the defining industry in the 21st Century, and thus the place where real job growth resides.

Let me ask you to do this: Calmly go to your computer, log onto 2GreenEnergy, search for and find this post, and send it (or the link to EnergyFactCheck.org) to someone who, for whatever reason, doesn't seem to get this. It will make you feel good. And that's a promise – from me.

# May I Ask a Favor of You Re: the CleanTech Industry, Please?

I was hoping that I could ask you a favor. As the editor of 2GreenEnergy, I'm constantly looking for new business models and strategies, and, like anyone, I focus on areas that seem to be good fits for my capabilities.

Sure, there are aspects of the clean energy industry that yield great success for people in endeavors like selling rooftop solar PV, renting e-bikes, designing LEED-certified buildings, etc. But personally, I have no particular skills that would distinguish me in any of these arenas.

Having said, that, I do have a few assets that I can bring to the table:

- A capability, demonstrated over a period of several decades, to solve some of the world's thorniest business problems that are related to the marketing/popularization of technology.

- Understanding of the science underpinning renewable energy, and sustainability more generally.

- Passion for ethical business, and a commitment to the welfare of humankind.

- A reasonable level of ability to express business/technology concepts in writing.

Now, let me ask you this: What activities within the sphere of the cleantech industry require all or most of these? I've spent untold hours pondering that question, and, while I've come up with some answers that have generated some solid results, I'm always on the prowl for new and better ideas.

Maybe I'm so close to the problem that I struggle to see a solution that's right in front of my face. If you have an idea that might help, I'd sure appreciate hearing about it.

# A Few Suggestions for the United States on Her Birthday

It's Independence Day here in the United States—a good time to celebrate the marvels that this country represents, in particular, rule of law, and a meaningful constitution that generally protects the liberties of its individual citizens. The 4th of July is also a great opportunity to understand where the U.S. needs to go in order to make sure that these liberties extend to all people, and that they are not eroded over time. To that end, here are four suggestions:

1) Repeal all laws that flagrantly violate the Constitution, e.g., the National Defense Authorization Act. Among its other offensive aspects, the NDAA allows the U.S. military to detain indefinitely persons who are deemed to commit "belligerent acts" against the United States. Insofar as there is no qualification of the term "belligerent acts," this renders void any notion of personal liberty; it nullifies both the 4th and 5th Amendments to the U.S. Constitution, as well as the natural rights of Americans. This is a shameful and frightening law, and it should particularly infuriate the many millions of brave soldiers and their families who have sacrificed so greatly to maintain our freedom.

2) On a related note, restore the basic notion of habeas corpus in all our dealings. We seem to feel that we can hold enemy combatants for decades without charging them with a crime or allowing them to challenge their imprisonment, even though Supreme Court rulings in 2004, 2006 and 2008 confirmed that prisoners at Guantánamo Bay do have habeas rights.

3) Overturn "Citizens United," the U.S. Supreme Court ruling that enables corporations to spend as much as they wish to decide on the outcome of our elections. If you think this isn't a real issue, ask yourself how it's possible that 89% of American voters want extended background checks for prospective gun owners, but

Congress refuses to pass such legislation. It's hard to imagine what our Founding Fathers would have said about a democracy that has become so twisted by the power of corporate profits that it renders mute the will of the common man; let's stay on the safe side and say it wouldn't be cause for celebration.

4) Take the moral high ground on the key environmental issues of the day. America's position as the most powerful force on Earth commands the respect of the rest of the world, and this confers an obligation to behave so as to forward the cause of human rights globally. Of course, there are hundreds of implications here, but at a minimum, it means reducing the horrific impact of humankind's actions on our oceans, our atmosphere, etc.

In 1835, French political thinker and historian Alexis de Tocqueville observed, "America is great because she is good. If America ceases to be good, America will cease to be great." Something to think about on our nation's birthday.

# Ah, Come On — Can't the Earth Be an "After Planet?"

Today is the anniversary of the first well-known UFO sighting in 1947, a good time to ask readers to ponder the most obvious question related to this phenomenon: Are we alone in the universe?

Dr. Michio Kaku, the ubiquitous physics professor and author, thinks we aren't; in fact, he classifies extraterrestrial civilizations according to the source they use to generate the energy they need. A Class I civilization derives its energy from its local star, where a Class II civilization (as I recall) somehow pulls energy out of its entire galaxy. While this way sounds a bit wild for some people to take seriously, considering our current lack of any experience with any beings whatsoever from other worlds, it carries with it an important implication, i.e., we're still a "Class 0 society."

Having said that, we're tantalizingly close to a big, fat promotion. The U.S. grid mix is about 5% solar PV and wind (both of which come from the sun), and this figure is growing every day. While 5% isn't huge, it's certainly worth talking about. Note that almost all of it has come online over the very recent past, and, further, that it's poised for exponential growth.

Think for a moment of the ads we see for weight loss, hair restoration, and home improvement that feature "before" and "after" photos. (Thankfully, the makers of ads for erectile dysfunction cures take a different tack.)

We're knocking on the door; let's get it done.

# Those Whose "Hearts Are Open" See the Need for Clean Energy

The emcee at a dance recital I attended yesterday began by calling for the audience to observe a moment of silence to honor our fallen war heroes. "Please open your hearts," he asked us as he closed his eyes and solemnly bowed his head. When he concluded his introductory remarks a few moments later, he asked, "Are your hearts still open? I hope so, for that's the best way to receive what you're about to experience here this afternoon."

I was quite moved by this, and I noted to myself that the concept of an open heart is one of the major reasons to care about the clean energy movement and what it's attempting to accomplish: a quality of life for everyone on this planet now, as well as those yet to be born.

What's interesting, though, is that this "open heart" notion is only one of many reasons to get onboard. What if your interest in renewable energy is patriotism, and you want to make sure the country you love succeeds economically in an international marketplace that has a huge appetite for "new energy" solutions? Maybe you're concerned that our fossil fuel-based approach to energy will cause water and food shortages, that in turn will create global political instability and force the most threatened countries to react militarily. Perhaps you don't want to be on the receiving end of terrorism, and you're concerned that our dependence on fossil fuels continues to empower the world's most evil people. What if you don't want to be one of the increasing number of victims of the various types of lung disease that are associated with breathing the aromatics of coal-fired power plants and the exhaust from vehicles powered by internal combustion engines?

If you meet any of these criteria, or dozens of others I could name, you have at least one good reason–maybe more–to support the migration to renewable energy.

Of course, if your heart is open at the same time, so much the better.

## Attitudes on Energy Policy Changing at Glacial Speeds

Last week, Charlie Rose presented this summary of a report which laid out how the melting of the Western Antarctic Ice Sheet is "beyond the point of no return," reminding us of the grim consequences: the slow but significant rise in the earth's sea levels.

I always wonder when I come across scientific findings like these: what does the common American think about stuff like this? In particular, how long will we go on, month after month, year after year, with reports like these piling up around us, before we tell our leadership to develop an energy policy that makes sense, given the realities of climate change (and the other issues associated with the burning of fossil fuels: ocean acidification, loss of biodiversity, increasing rates of cancer, etc.)?

I'm afraid the answer is that our attitudes towards climate change are shifting at the same pace that the glaciers themselves are melting: slowly. If we're making progress here, at this rate, it's happening over a period of decades.

Why? The answer may be summed up in another event in the mainstream American media this week: Republican presidential hopeful Marco Rubio's confident assertion that "the overwhelming scientific consensus on climate change is false. Rubio, highly regarded by almost half of U.S. voters, was unable to cite any sources for his skepticism, but the absence of any facts behind his belief doesn't make him any less credible among his many tens of millions of supporters.

The bottom line: a frighteningly large percentage of us put more stock in the speeches of politicians who act at the behest of their huge campaign donors than we do in the peer-reviewed publications of many thousands of our top scientists. Until that changes, we may find ourselves "stuck in neutral" with respect to our energy policy — or perhaps, under the circumstances, a more apt term may be "treading water."

## The Campaign to Discredit Clean Energy Can Only Intensify

I had lunch yesterday at the American Wind Energy Association conference with an interesting gentleman who, quite successfully from what I could discern, develops PV and wind projects in the U.S. and Latin America. The actual business model varies: where sometimes his team and he might sell the entire project when it's shovel-ready, in other cases they like to retain an interest. A typical wind project might be 100 MW or so, where the usual PV effort is a fraction of that, perhaps a couple of MW.

He mentioned something that I thought I'd offer readers: an explanation of the fairly recent ruckus being raised about the government subsidies for solar and wind. "Why," he asked me in a thoughtful tone, "do you think Fox News and congressional Republicans waited until now before starting their campaign to convince voters that renewable energy is a waste of money, a drain on the economy, a job-killer, part of a socialist agenda, etc.? The tax credits have been around for quite a while. Virtually everyone on both sides of the aisle were absolutely *fine* on this until very recently."

"Well," I replied, "My personal theory is that, when all this was in its infancy, no one thought it was worth the effort that would have been required to kill it. It wasn't really a threat to the fossil fuel industry, and no one believed that it could possibly become one. Now, with wind at almost 5% of the national grid mix, and growing steadily, it's a threat in a big way."

"That's exactly right," he nodded. "Neither the fossil fuel boys nor the utilities saw this coming. They thought it was likely to go nowhere, and they figured they could simply ignore it. It turns out that this was a *huge* mistake for them. At this point their situation is especially dire, when you think about it, because the costs of PV and wind have fallen so dramatically. The cost of electricity from a natural gas project may be $60/MWh; my last wind project was at $22 with the PTC (production tax credit) — but even without the PTC, it's still under $50. So now the gloves are off; it's really going to get ugly."

I'm afraid this guy is spot on. As the mid-term elections in the U.S. get closer, and 2016 right behind, watch what happens in terms of rhetoric, and the efforts to squash renewable energy. Keep an eye on legislative efforts to repeal RPSs (renewable portfolio standards), declaw the EPA, put an axe through tax incentives for solar and wind, get rid of net-metering provisions, and kill ARPA-E funding of cleantech R&D.

My prediction, sadly, is that nothing of any real value to a healthy environment will be exempt.

## We Should Help Our Top Corporations Embrace Sustainability

Obviously, a great deal of immorality exists in both our public and private sectors. Whether we're talking about the purveyors of junk food, cigarettes, assault weapons, clothing made by children, or, more familiarly, an energy playing field that favors oil and coal, it's common for certain big corporations to behave badly, while buying favors from government to support their evil undertakings.

The question then becomes: What does one do about this? While there's no easy answer, personally, I'm willing to help corporations change direction for the better, and, I'm happy to report, there are plenty that wish to do exactly that. I know Lockheed Martin builds war machines and coal processing equipment. But now they're getting into renewable energy, and, with annual revenues of $47 billion, when they do something, they do it in a big way. I have no compunction helping the Lockheed Martins of the world change their focus from destructive to constructive activities and products.

That's why I took them up on their invitation and visited their facility in Virginia a few months ago in which they have (really cool) demonstrations of what they're trying to get done in ocean thermal energy conversion and half a dozen other clean energy technologies. I sent them a few items from our list of clean energy investment opportunities, and they're taking a long look at a few.

I have friends who can't understand this, who say that I should stay away from historically bad actors. I'm not convinced; in fact, I don't think that makes any more sense than the assertion that churches shouldn't accept sinners.

I even have contacts at Dow Chemical. Historically, it doesn't get much more morally obnoxious than Dow, unless you have some warped appreciation for agent orange and napalm, two products that caused countless thousands of agonizing deaths, while making their shareholders extremely wealthy over the last half century. But now, Dow wants to look to sustainability and eco-friendliness in the chemical industry, and they want my advice on how to get there. I'm happy to oblige.

If we stay away from the organizations that have the greatest potential to change the world for the better, we're missing an important opportunity.

# A Few Ideas for Those Who Want To Make a Difference Re: Sustainability

I thought readers might be interested in this note I just sent to an old friend who's getting on in years and has become concerned that humankind has gotten off the track vis-a-vis sustainability. As a man of reason and compassion, he wants to use a healthy chunk of his life savings to make a difference in the outcome. When he asked for my advice, I gave him a few ideas, which I summarized in the email below.

Per our talk yesterday, here are a few ideas by which you can make a difference in creating a sustainable future for your grandchildren and the rest of humankind.

*Invest!* As I mentioned, I have reviewed well over 2000 cleantech concepts since the inception of my website (2GreenEnergy.com) and I have selected the best ones to promote on my page for cleantech investors. At your convenience, I'd be happy to chat at whatever level of detail you like about any that pique your interest.

*Donate!* We also discussed, the real bogeyman facing humankind is runaway population in the developing world. For humanitarians, a key issue is the alleviating of their suffering, as these people live in terrible conditions. But, in addition, literally everyone on Earth suffers as a result of their activities, which include deforestation (slashing and burning the woodlands for fuel as heating, lighting, and cooking). On a per kilowatt-hour basis, this is *by far* the dirtiest form of energy known to humanity.

If there is a chance to deal with this problem effectively, it lies in providing education, especially for women. To put it bluntly, educated women don't have 15 kids; they have smaller, healthier, and more stable families. One of my favorite organizations operating in this space is The Turimiquire Foundation, specializing in education and family planning in Northern Venezuela. Another is The Eleos

Foundation (based near us in Montecito, CA), which, albeit a non-profit, is really about "conscious capitalism"; the group doesn't take donations per se, but rather investments in new businesses that are started by budding entrepreneurs, mostly in Africa, whose missions are to provide health and educational services to the BOP (bottom of pyramid).

*Advocate!* We also talked about the fact that, in the U.S. at least, corruption is the norm in terms of law-making in Washington. Of course, it may be far worse in places like India, and I really don't have an answer there. But I do here at home.

The reason our leaders have no incentive to do what's right for the American people is that our interests are essentially irrelevant to them. They're elected with huge campaign contributions from corporate interests, and then, when they're no longer in office, they (in 85% of cases, anyway) become lobbyists in the industries that they served while in Washington. As long as this remains the case, we would be very foolish to expect fair-minded, responsible lawmaking to support the true needs of the people.

The first thing to do here is to overturn the U.S. Supreme Court decision "Citizens United," which enables corporations to spend as much as they want to influence our elections in whatever direction they choose. Fortunately, there is a large and growing number of grass-roots efforts in this space that are steadily gaining traction. Bernie Sanders (I-VT) is sponsoring an initiative called "Saving American Democracy." Perhaps my favorite approach, however, is led by a fellow I've met and interviewed on my radio show, David Cobb, green party presidential candidate in 2004; it's called "Move To Amend." These folks most certainly accept donations, and they use them judiciously to spread the word.

Again, I appreciate the fact that you're one of the "good guys," and I know that you'll be effective at helping here.

# What Science Can Tell Us – And What It Can't

I've always enjoyed helping my kids with their homework, and, as they've gotten older, I've been learning a great deal myself from what I'm helping them study. Last night, I spent a few happy hours helping my son Jake study for a botany test, during which I came across something rather surprising: many of the uses that plants have for their essential micronutrients – elements like chlorine, iron, manganese, copper, cobalt, zinc, molybdenum and boron are "not well understood." I.e., we know they're important, albeit in concentrations of a few parts per million, but we're not sure exactly why, and neither do we understand the transport mechanisms for these nutrients that are active within the organism.

Until I read this, I would have expected that very little would remain unknown to the top minds in plant biochemistry as we make our way into the 21st Century, but apparently that's not the case. I would have thought that the only real mysteries remaining in science are the freaky, counter-intuitive aspects of the world at the cosmological level, e.g., dark energy, or in the infinitesimally small world, e.g., quantum entanglement. I also acknowledge that we're a very long way from having our wits wrapped around the nature of consciousness.

So let us ask ourselves: Will science eventually bring us the answers we desire so intensely, or will certain aspects of the world around us forever remain elusive? I'm reminded of a debate on science and religion in which Neil deGrasse Tyson's opponent challenged the popular astrophysicist, "So, you're saying that dark energy and dark matter are far more pervasive in the universe than the content that science claims to understand. Couldn't that unknown stuff be God?" Tyson responded, "Sure. But if your belief in God is hinged on what science doesn't understand at this moment in time, you need to realize that you're standing on an island that's getting smaller every year. A few centuries ago, we thought that thunder, earthquakes, famines, and disease were God's way of expressing His displeasure with our sinful ways. With the advent of modern science, all of that ignorance is gone, and it's gone forever."

If we accept Tyson's reasoning, we might conclude that science will eventually leave no aspect of our existence unanswered. I'm not so sure. While I refrain from taking a public stand on religion, I will say this about science: My bet is that humanity's quest to understand the essential nature of the universe will not succeed. There is no reason to believe that a species that evolved over the last 200,000 years, stuck, as we are, with senses that are limited to three spatial dimensions, can grasp realities that obviously are not bound by this constraint. We were evolved to hunt mastodons and grow corn, not to unravel string theory or whatever lies beyond that — theories that require us to intuit the world in 11 dimensions.

Having said that, let's ask ourselves how important, in the scheme of things, the quest for this ultimate understanding of the universe actually is, and evaluate two threats:

1. Our civilization will suffer from an ongoing ignorance of the ultimate building blocks of matter and of the origins of the universe.

   or

2. Our civilization will suffer a horrific breakdown due to our unrestrained over-consumption of resources.

Clearly, we should be far more worried about the latter.

# We Need An Energy Policy

A friend sent me a newspaper story about his local (Philadelphia) region: "Offshore Wind Farm Rejected in New Jersey." Rightfully, he's dismayed.

The analysis here shows how flawed our whole approach is to providing energy to businesses and consumers. The entire thing needs to be ripped out by the roots, and replaced by an energy policy at the federal level (we have none at all now) that points in the direction we as a nation want to take, and contains a few main tenets:

- Utilities need to phase out fossil fuels over the coming decades; the first priority here is decommissioning coal-fired power plants. In particular, we should be providing incentives that will encourage utilities to generate power from no-carbon resources (especially renewables), and implement smart-grid, energy storage, high-voltage transmission over large distances, and integration of the three major grids in the U.S.

- Municipalities need to have incentives to reduce the energy impact on transportation: more/better mass transit, encouraging fewer vehicle miles driven. They should also be encouraged to implement "smart cities," which is itself multi-faceted.

- At the "load" (energy consumer) level, we need to provide incentives that will encourage conservation, efficiency, distributed generation, and electric transportation. The new approach needs to deal with the "death spiral" facing utilities, where consumers leave the grid, driving up the costs for the remaining utility customers, encouraging even more consumers to leave the grid.

All of this can and should be revenue-neutral. We have every right to create a level playing field that will make all this happen naturally, taxing behavior that has a deleterious effect on the environment, and rewarding behavior that takes us in the direction of sustainability. It's really not rocket-science, and I really don't think it's all that controversial. Does anyone who studies the subject even superficially really believe we can carry on indefinitely with the status quo?

In fact, I'm hoping the phone rings right now and U.S. Energy Secretary Ernie Moniz tells me he wants me to come to Washington to help him make all this happen — but I'm not holding my breath.

# Electric Transportation and Carbon Dioxide

I just received this:

*Today, Ford announced its decision to use GE charging stations for its workplace charging network. Ford plans to install the GE WattStation™ at more than 50 of its facilities throughout 2014. The stations will be networked together, allowing Ford to gather information such as the number of hours vehicles are charging and the amount of carbon dioxide reduced.*

I'm always amused when people who should know better make statements to the effect that they know how much $CO_2$ is reduced as they charge their EVs. This figure, sometimes positive, other times negative, fluctuates in real-time throughout the day and night as grid operators around the nation figure out how they can meet ever-changing demand at the lowest cost, and then buy and sell power from different sources accordingly. This is further complicated by the fact that, even within one type of resource, say coal, there are numerous variables in terms of plant efficiencies, losses in transmission, coal types, levels of effectiveness of scrubbing, etc. — none of which we can monitor with any accuracy.

And I chose coal deliberately, as, especially in that part of the country (Dearborn, Michigan), an incremental load on the grid almost always means burning more coal, which is far worse for the environment and human health, not only in terms of $CO_2$, but also NOx, SOx, heavy metals, radioactive isotopes, etc., than the oil that the EV displaced.

That said, I remain a fan of electric transportation, as I believe that overall, we're moving in the right direction in terms of all the things that will make EVs a terrific solution going forward. Not only are we decommissioning coal, but we're also bringing on more renewable energy, and since that comes largely in the form of solar and wind, it means integrating variable resources. EVs, through their ability to store excess energy capacity, will be a huge help in this regard over time.

Also, we need to keep in mind that many people install solar on their roofs when they get an EV, totally eliminating this issue. In fact, the third quarter of 2013 saw the largest number of American homes in history (31,000) install solar panels on their rooftops. This is the most recent data I have; there could have been new records set in the two more recent quarters.

We'll get there. That's not the issue, but rather this: How much damage will we have done in the process? The answer: *no one knows.*

## A Few Individuals Can Make a Huge Difference

Each day we watch the slow grind of the forces that shape our world in terms of environmental justice. We ask ourselves questions that have no answers currently: How much of the Amazon rain forest will we be able to preserve? Will the migration away from fossil fuels occur in time to save the Greenland Ice Sheet? Will Chevron eventually be forced to pay for the devastation it caused in Ecuador? Phenomena like these, unfolding as they are–not across months or years–but over a period of decades, are why the destruction of our natural environment is often referred to as a "train-wreck in slow motion."

Given all this, it's easy to forget that each one of us plays an important role in the outcome, and that a few key individuals have single-handedly brought about huge redirections in the course of humankind—even previously unknown and indistinguished people like the Chinese man who defied the armored tanks in Tienanmen

Square in 1989, or the young fellow who lighted himself on fire, bringing on the Arab Spring in 2010.

Speaking of individuals who changed our civilization, let's consider Voltaire, a man who was anything but indistinguished. According to the Writer's Almanac, last Tuesday marked the anniversary of the

*"....day in 1778 that Voltaire returned to Paris after living in exile for 28 years in protest against France's religious fanaticism. He was a crusader for human rights and one of the most respected people in Europe. When he was allowed to return home, more than 300 people came to visit him his first day in the city. One of those visitors was Benjamin Franklin, fresh from helping to lead the revolution in the United States of America. Franklin had brought his grandson with him and asked Voltaire to bless the little boy."*

When you look at the horrors that Muslim extremists are wreaking around the world, and on their own people (especially women), remind yourself of one of the fundamental reasons for all this mayhem: that this part of the world never received the fruits of what Voltaire and just a few others brought us: the Age of Reason/the Enlightenment, the French Revolution, the U.S. Declaration of Independence, the Bill of Rights, and so forth. Keep in mind how radical these ideas were in their time, and how limited our human rights would be without them.

Then consider what we all can do to bring about a *new* Enlightenment— one that respects the basic rights of all seven billion of us, as well as the health and sustainability of the natural environment.

# Sustainability and the Arc of the Moral Universe

During a 30-minute drive I took earlier today, I had the pleasure of listening to a 1964 talk that Dr. Martin Luther King, Jr. delivered at the Baccalaureate sermon at the commencement exercises for Wesleyan University in Middletown, Connecticut, which included that fabulous line: *"The arc of the moral universe is long, but it bends toward justice."* For what it's worth, this quote has a long and very interesting history, which I encourage readers to explore.

Yet regardless of its history, we'd all like to believe that its message is, in fact, true, insofar as it forms the basis of our optimism – at least our hope – that humankind can somehow find its way to a just, kind, and sustainable world.

The speech hit on several other related ideas, for example, the teachings of Jesus, Gandhi, the Quakers and so many others to the effect that we should love our enemies. King also mentioned Henry David Thoreau and the concept of civil disobedience, pointing out that we have the same moral obligation to oppose evil as we do to support good. Obviously, there are plenty of people in the sustainability movement who involve themselves in civil disobedience, and even more (including me) who participate in legal, non-violent protests against "environmental evil."

If you happen to be looking for a low-force way to get behind all of this, you may wish to consider what legendary environmentalist Bill McKibben recommends: divest. By simply refusing to own stock in companies whose businesses are based on raping the environment for profit, you are raising their cost of capital and making their job that much tougher. And how hard is that? You don't have to risk arrest, or even walk around chanting and carrying a placard. Just be one of the large and growing number of people and organizations that have sold their stock in the fossil fuel industry, or find another way to demonstrate your concern for the long-term success of the human race. It's easy as pie.

# To Achieve a Sustainable Approach to Energy We Need a Plan

In a discussion I had yesterday with an old friend and long-time 2GreenEnergy subscriber, I was reminded of how outrageous it is that the United States has no energy policy. Is it really any wonder we're making such dreadfully slow progress in the direction of a sustainable approach to energy, considering that we don't know where we're going?

What's the matter with asking our leaders to chart out the next few decades, and put a stick in the ground re: our phasing out of fossil fuels? Where do we want to be in three years? 30? Isn't that what leaders do, i.e., lead?

When you listen to our great energy pundits (e.g., Amory Lovins) present, this subject is 99% of the presentation, i.e., how, exactly, it is possible to bring together energy conservation, efficiency in its dozens of forms, and the different flavors of renewables, each with its steadily rising effectiveness and falling cost curve – all flowing together to eliminate fossil fuels over the coming few decades. I've met Lovins a couple of times after talks he's given, and trust me, he's pretty convincing. What's the problem with adopting some sort of strategy along these lines?

Of course, we may not hit every target along the way; personally, I won't be upset if we meet occasional setbacks. In my estimation, it's far better to deal with failure and make mid-course corrections than not to try at all.

I'm reminded of this snappy little conversation that Lewis Carroll crafted for Alice and the Cheshire Cat. Alice begins by asking:

*"Would you tell me, please, which way I ought to go from here?"*

*"That depends a good deal on where you want to get to."*

*"I don't much care where –"*

*"Then it doesn't matter which way you go."*

We're amused at this clever absurdity, but this is precisely what we're doing with our energy policy.

## "60 Minutes" Airs Hatchet-Job on CleanTech

The CBS news show "60 Minutes" sports a history of hatchet-jobs that goes back almost half a century. They're phenomenally good at selecting a certain conclusion and then supporting it with misleading reporting, trick camera-work, and quotes taken out of context.

Last Sunday's segment on the demise of the cleantech industry was a beautiful case in point. People all over America came away with the idea that this business sector is dying — or dead — and, worse, that they, the rank-and-file U.S. citizen had been duped into paying for the failure with their tax dollars.

But couldn't these handsome, smiling faces at CBS have made even the faintest attempt at fairness? They dredged up the story of Solyndra, the government-backed failure in which the all-powerful enemies of clean energy take such delight, then informed the audience about six or seven other losses.

But what about the numerous successes?

What about the imperative to develop cleantech in the first place, by virtue of things like climate change, ocean acidification, and lung disease? In 15 long minutes, there was not a single mention made of any of this.

What about the importance of American competitiveness in a global economy in which clean energy is clearly becoming an extremely important (arguably the single most dominant) industry?

What about the private sector, where the biggest banks in the known universe: Credit Suisse, Deutsche Bank, Citigroup, etc. are currently investing seven trillion dollars (that's not a typo, nor a mistake; it's trillions of dollars) of private capital?

Couldn't CBS have noted what the solar PV industry did last year? The "TAN – Guggenhein ETF (Exchange-Traded Fund)" – the benchmark for the solar PV industry — was up a mere 129.64% in 2013. That's not exactly moribund by my accounting. I don't know what *your* portfolio did last year, but *mine* sure as hell wasn't up 129%. Wasn't any of this worth a single mention?

How about the fact the wind and solar industries are *twice* the size they were four years ago?

Mightn't they have mentioned that the portion of grants given to ventures that later failed represented less than 3% of the total portfolio?

What about an even more basic fact? Three-quarters of *all* businesses fail — whether they're in cleantech or healthcare or pizza, whether they're government-backed or not.

I struggle to think of anything more irresponsible than fabricating a case like this and convincing tens of millions of innocent and credulous Americans who happen not to follow this subject closely, each sitting attentively in their living rooms all over this great nation, that cleantech is a failure, that they got ripped off, and that government malice or stupidity is to blame. That's outrageously shameful stuff, but hey, 60 Minutes has been doing this quite successfully since 1968; I should have come to expect it by now.

"Simply put, 60 Minutes is flat wrong on the facts," U.S. Department of Energy spokesman Bill Gibbons said in an emailed statement, as if it's an accident, or as if this is the the first time this happened. He went on to explain, "The clean energy economy in America is real and we are increasingly competitive in this rapidly-expanding global industry. This is a race we can, must and will win."

Good going, Bill. You said it well — and you managed to put it more calmly than I did (which is why you're a DoE spokesperson and I'm not).

I'd love to have some insight into the decision-making that goes on at CBS, and I'll close with two quick points on this:

1) Lesley Stahl's net worth is estimated at $20 million. She's extremely intelligent and talented, but if she had a conscience, wouldn't she have told the producer of the show to take a hike when he came to her with this concept? She wouldn't exactly be working at Walmart if she did. I find it extraordinary that wealthy people like this toe the line to the demands of their higher-ups, at the expense of compromising what little's left of their integrity.

2) As I mentioned above, it's clear that the CBS brass picks its conclusions, and then goes about the task of supporting them. When the whole production is ready to air, their piece isn't good; it's not excellent; it's *perfect*. Any viewer with the IQ of a turnip will be obliged to agree with whatever they happen to be selling at the moment. What's the point of deliberately, with such totally admirable precision, killing the cleantech industry? Who stands to gain?

Wait a second; you don't think.......?

# Happy Birthday Spinoza, Perhaps History's Greatest Radical

It's the birthday (1632) of the philosopher Baruch Spinoza, whose most important ideas, according to the Writer's Almanac, were that "everything in the universe is made of a single substance, and that everything in the universe is subject to natural laws. He also argued that the soul and the body are not really separate, but two parts of the same thing. He believed that God did not stand outside the universe, but rather that the universe itself was God, and that everything in the universe was perfect and divine."

One can see how radical thinking like this got him into hot water with the church in the 17th Century. But I find it interesting that even in the face of all our scientific advancements, some of Spinoza's 350-year-old ideas may turn out to be correct. I'm sure the chemists who developed the periodic table in the 19th Century regarded Spinoza as a quaint old whack-job, but he doesn't seem so whacky now that we understand quarks and string theory, does he? And obviously, the religious people – of his day and our own – recoil at the notion that the soul and the body are two parts of the same thing. But if you ask a scientist today for the accepted modern theory of human consciousness, be prepared for a rude shock: the old dualities of mind/body or soul/body are no longer in place.

Radical thinking, i.e., serious exploration that takes all the paradigms of the day and tosses them out the window, is actually quite difficult, and for that reason, it's something I deeply respect. This is why I'm always happy to talk with anyone who claims to have an idea that appears to violate the laws of physics as we understand them.

Having said that, I place the bar quite high. Someone who wants to raise money to build a prototype of a machine that spits out more power than it consumes, thus violating the first and second laws of thermodynamics, merits this extremely quick, 26-word conversation: "That's interesting, though theoretically impossible. But if you can build a working model on your own, and send me a video, let's have a follow-on discussion." Of course, this is seldom the end of the conversation, as, inevitably, the guy feels compelled to convince me that he's right and I'm wrong. Here, I respond with another 12 words, bringing the grand total to 38: "Sorry. I don't want to hear it; I want to see it."

So far, I'm batting exactly zero on those "follow-on discussions," but I continue undeterred in my quest to find the next Spinoza.

# Hot Times in Tucson for Renewable Energy – La Cucaracha!

This afternoon I was reminded of an important fact: the promotional work that authors of renewable energy books do isn't always relaxing, fun, and productive. I (foolishly?) had agreed to do an hour-long ultra-right-wing talk radio show in Tucson, AZ. The conversation with the host, Charles Heller, was completely civil, though we really didn't agree on too much.

It got more interesting when we took calls from listeners, who, as one can only imagine, are apparently all climate change denier zealots, and trust me, they didn't cotton to me. One guy was so angry with me I could almost see his clenched fists trembling; in fact, he was so enraged he could barely speak, but eventually made a statement that he finished up by calling me a "cockroach."

Oh my.

I took a deep breath and calmly explained that I'm simply a guy who speaks with a great number of scientists, and trusts what they tell me. I believe in the theory of evolution, the big bang, quantum mechanics and so forth — not because I've independently verified them, but because I don't believe there's a better way to get at the truth on matters like these than to accept the findings of highly intelligent people who have studied these subjects their entire lives. I know many of these people personally, and the idea that all these university professors and the like have formed a giant conspiracy to perpetrate the largest hoax in human history doesn't hold water with me.

I concluded, "If that makes me a cockroach, I'm afraid I don't know what to tell you."

Charles, buddy, what'd'ya say?   Perhaps we could take our next caller???

Oscar Wilde once said, "The only bad publicity is an obituary." It's hard to argue with that, but appearing on shows like this has no value for me – or anyone. Charles (who gentlemanly demanded that the caller retract his "cockroach" comment) wants me back on another show.  But — sorry Charles — this is pointless.

# Prediction: Obama Will Axe the Keystone XL Pipeline

I have a good feeling that U.S. President Obama will axe the Keystone XL Pipeline. My reasoning has nothing to do with the noise that environmentalists are making, though I'm not discounting that effect altogether. I'm thinking that none of the other things he seems to want to get accomplished currently (having passed the Affordable Care Act) have any chance of happening. Congress shot gun control dead and said "adios" to immigration reform. What about a grand bargain? Are you serious?

Nixing the pipeline is something Obama can actually make happen. From what I can see, he's unimpressed with the job-creation numbers (it's only a few dozen after the project is in place), and he doesn't believe (nor do I) that there is solid logic and moral justification behind the idea that we should go ahead with the plan because the environmental devastation associated with all that dirty oil is going to happen whether we're involved in it or not. Kids can buy drugs whether I sell them or not, but that doesn't justify my selling them.

Killing the pipeline will enable Obama to take the moral high ground, and show that the largest economy on Earth is proactively weaning itself off fossil fuels. In turn, this could set the stage for an international agreement on the subject – something that looked impossible a few years ago.

Doesn't there simply have to be a decent denouement to the presidency of this guy, whom we ushered into office with such gusto in 2008?

If he pulls this off, I'll try my best to forgive his inexplicable behavior on Guantanamo Bay, the fascist National Defense Authorization Act, drone warfare, the rabid prosecution of whistle-blowers – each one by itself jaw-dropping — things of which no one ever dreamed him capable when we elected him.

This would be the most stunning victory for a world leader in a very long time — arguably in all human history. Astonishingly, Obama won the Nobel Peace Prize. Now he can earn it.

# Attempting To View Renewable Energy Intelligently

It's the birthday of F. Scott Fitzgerald, whose affinity for the leisure class served as the driving force behind many of the classics he produced in the early 20th Century. Somewhere along the way, Fitzgerald wrote something that I've always treasured: "The test of a first-rate intelligence is the ability to hold two opposed ideas in the mind at the same time, and still retain the ability to function."

It's the lack of the "first-rate intelligence" that lies at the root of so many problems in the world today. We want easy answers; we want to see things in black and white terms, but factually, today's world doesn't present itself that way; life in the 21st Century is more nuanced.

I aspire to that sort of intelligence (though I certainly don't claim to have achieved it). My evolving viewpoints on renewable energy are an example of my unexceptional attempts to reach this point. I'm a clean energy advocate, obviously, though I try not to lose sight of the "tough realities" – as I like to call them:

- There are places where the availability of renewable resources is terribly weak.

- How well and how quickly can we develop the peripheral technologies that will help us integrate large volumes of solar and wind (given that they're variable in nature): smart grid, low-cost energy storage, high-voltage transmission, vehicle-to-grid, etc.?

- How far in the direction of a sustainable approach to energy can we get with the real "low-hanging fruit," i.e., energy efficiency and conservation?

- What's the trajectory for other appealing but not-yet-available technologies, e.g., thorium (nuclear) reactors?

- What's to be done with the enormous and fabulously expensive infrastructure we have in place currently to process fossil fuels?

- We can't snap our fingers and get all the lobbyists for the oil companies out of our law-making process. Among other things this means that, realistically, fossil fuels will continue to enjoy preferential treatment over renewables, despite their ill-effects on our health and environment.

- I advocate in favor of democracy too, but here in the U.S., voters are deluged with inflammatory messages every two years about their *current* situation, not their *future*, and so they disdain energy solutions that would suggest even a tiny compromise in their consumer life-style *today*.

This makes for an extremely complicated calculus that, actually, forces us to keep not *two*, but *several* opposing ideas in our heads simultaneously.

If you have an idea on expanding humankind's level of this so-called "first-rate intelligence," I'd certainly love to hear from you.

# Renewable Energy Nay-sayers

Obviously, renewable energy has a whole host of nay-sayers who make a variety of points, including:

- It's expensive. (This is true, though it's becoming less so each day – and it depends on how one does the accounting. Some of us think we should assign a value to human health, biodiversity, and the natural environment — at which point clean energy becomes the deal of the century.)

- It relies on variable resources. (Again, this is true, but at the rate we're integrating it now, that variability has very little effect, and energy storage looks increasingly viable as we go forward.)

- It hasn't made a significant dent in the energy supply. (That can be argued, though realize that wind was over 4% of our grid-mix in the U.S. last year, which is nothing at which to sneeze. Also, let's keep this in perspective: Coal has been used for heating since the cave man, and archeologists are still digging up evidence of the way coal was used by the Romans in the first few centuries CE. More recently, the fossil fuel boys and the mega-corporations behind them have been doing their thing on an aggressive, for-profit basis for 200 years. Is renewable energy expected to clean up a mess in a few years that six generations of robber barons and latter-day Wall Street profiteers took two full centuries to create?)

As a clean energy advocate, I'm quite inspired with the progress the industry has made, and I'm proud to be a part of it.

## Talking Renewable Energy on a Conservative Radio Talk-Show

An old friend from high school has invited me to be a guest on his radio show which takes a conservative perspective on the topics of the day. I'll be on for an hour to talk to him and entertain callers' questions about my views on renewable energy, electric transportation, and sustainability more generally. When he called to schedule the interview, he promised that the talk wouldn't be combative, i.e., he won't call me a communist, a bleeding heart, etc.

I had to choke back my laughter when he announced these conditions: "You don't know the hundreds of other similar situations in which I've found myself over the years. Most of the talk radio shows that have had me on have callers from hell, and a few of them were hosted by right-wing attack dogs themselves. There is literally nothing you could say or ask that could possibly offend me."

The position of a conservative-minded show, of course, is that government is bad, and that unfettered private enterprise is good – and those who know me understand that I'm not wholly opposed to this viewpoint; I've been a business owner almost my entire adult life, and I understand the value of taking responsibility for my own condition in life. I simply think the situation isn't as black and white as the ideologues paint it to be.

In the particular case of this upcoming radio show, I'm guessing that the concept is that renewable energy is receiving subsidies, therefore it's part of the plan of our president (a Kenyan-born Muslim socialist) to cripple private enterprise through ever-increasing regulation, and, ultimately, to get as many Americans as possible on food stamps. OK, I'm oversimplifying. Maybe. We'll see.

But I thought readers might be interested in a few of my "talking points," starting with a few of our government's intrusion into transportation:

- Yes, government is pushing industry for better fuel economy and alternative fuels; it's playing a role in the transportation of the 21st Century, just like it did in the 20th, when it subsidized domestic oil exploration, built the roads and highways, and consistently deployed the military to maintain access to oil from foreign sources.

- We shouldn't lose sight of the fact that our tax-payers are still writing checks in the amount of tens of billions of dollars annually to the oil companies, the most profitable industry in the history of the known universe, to make that business even more profitable. While the American voter hates this arrangement by a factor of approximately 70-30, he's completely powerless to change it. There's a word for that: corruption. It's the corruptive force of huge corporations, unchecked and unregulated, that has produced this outrageous ethical, economic, and environmental catastrophe.

- The involvement from government hasn't been the tragedy that the right wing promotes. Are our listeners aware that radar systems that came from government have virtually eliminated fatal accidents on our commercial airlines? The annual risk of being killed in a plane crash for the average American is about 1 in 11 million, as compared with the annual risk of being killed in a motor vehicle crash, which is more than 2000 times greater (approximately 1 in 5000).

- And speaking of the government and the automobile industry, how many of us know the source of every single safety advancement, from seat belts in 1961 to anti-lock braking, air-bags, and the many dozens of other technologies that save more lives each year (though each one was fought tooth-and-nail by the auto industry itself)?

- Whence came the effort to put a man on the moon and to start our journey of exploration of vast regions of the universe?

- Taking the subject of transportation back down to Earth, have we considered where the Internet came from, that provides us our real-time traffic maps, our roadside assistance, the backbone for deployment of emergency medical services, not to mention the hundreds of other benefits we count on every day?

Let's conclude this by saying that government's encouraging progressive concepts in transportation — pragmatic concepts that have proven themselves thousands of times over for their effectiveness in protecting your life and providing the safekeeping of your loved ones — are not entirely bad.

From there, let's branch out into a few ideas on the larger topic of what's happening regarding the destruction of our ecosystems and government's responsibility to take action to mitigate the disaster, i.e., to use common sense and rationality to restrain the private sector:

- Even the ultra-right-wing Cato Institute acknowledges the concept of anthropogenic climate change. Gone are the days when people who wish to be taken seriously can say that climate change is a hoax. So where do we go from there?

- Some say that our civilization is not duty-bound to take preventative measures against climate change because we don't have adequate visibility into the future. This does not hold water with me. Yes, we could be saved by a great number of things, e.g., a new technology or some unforeseeable event in the cosmos. But society's depending on the unknown to halt the destruction of our environment is not sane, responsible behavior.

- Some argue that, because the greatest damage from climate change will happen many decades hence, our imperative to mitigate that damage *itself* comes decades hence. This is a similarly unsupportable position; it has no more validity than an oncologist who discovers a small tumor on my lung but does not advise me to stop smoking, since the greatest part of the damage has not yet materialized.

I'm guessing that my host, a believer as he is in free-market capitalism, will assert that there exists a self-correcting mechanism that minimizes environmental damage on the basis that capitalism abhors waste. Again, this is specious. What capitalists abhor is wasting money, not CO2, or small but lethal quantities of heavy metals. The choice here isn't between wasting harmful byproducts of fossil fuels or not wasting them; it's between cleaning up the waste or not cleaning it up. We have adequate proof over the past two centuries that, when industrialists are unregulated, they most often choose not to clean up after themselves.

Lastly, I appeal to patriotism. If you really care about America, and I'm sure the vast majority of the show's listeners do, here are a few things to consider:

- Our addiction to oil causes us to borrow half a billion dollars a day and send it to our enemies. Our economic solvency declines at the same time that the strength and power of terrorists increases. If you understand this, and if you care about our national security, I think you're at a loss to defend an energy policy rooted in oil.

- The entire rest of the developed world understands something that we apparently do not: advanced solutions to energy are the defining industry in the 21st Century. We, as a nation, can pretend that alternative energy is a hoax, that it's an anti-capitalist plot, but doing so is nothing less than an invitation to China to hasten its ascent into the position as the leading economic (and military?) power. Why on Earth are we following this outrageously stupid and masochistic course? Again, it's corruption. Our government is owned by the oil companies, and guess what? You might care about American jobs and the quality of life for the 300 million of us, most of whom come from families who made sacrifices to keep all of us safe and free. But they don't, as long as they're maintaining their stranglehold on the world economy. Any real American should be mad as hell about this.

So what are the few remaining open issues? It really all boils down to this: In the absence of informed, enlightened people like you, dear reader, the private sector, if left alone, will happily suck the last molecule of crude out of the ground and mine the last lump of coal, and sell it to us. And, just as happily, we'll burn it to produce what we feel is our God-given right: cheap, abundant energy. Yes, the consequences will be catastrophic, but no one wants to hear that.

It was less than a year ago when the debate on the subject in the 2012 U.S. presidential election included only two ideas: Obama's "all of the above" strategy – make no enemies. Coal, nuclear, gas, renewables – let's regard them as equals. Romney's ridicule of anything but the very least-cost energy solution (fossil fuels) and the idea that we have some sort of obligation to protect our environment and long-term survival. The popular vote was very close (50%-47%), i.e., between the two, they received over 97% of the ballots cast.

So is my viewpoint popularly accepted? Hardly. But it is what it is. If this guy wants to attack me, he won't be the first, nor the last.

# If the Move To Renewables Is Inevitable, Why Not Do It Now?

Here's a question for you: When you listen to the debates in English Parliament, and hear how people with opposing viewpoints heckle and interrupt one another, doesn't your skin crawl? Mine does. These people have such incredible manners on most occasions, but not in public speaking. How is that possible?

When I saw an article in which British Prime Minister David Cameron scolded Europe for "missing out on the fracking boom," I could imagine the loud HARRUMPHs he must have received from the environmentalists.

It really is a very interesting argument. There are 200+ sovereign countries, each competing for economic prosperity on a globe with a fixed supply of resources. Those who restrain themselves for the sake of the planet's welfare are, indeed, at a disadvantage to those who rape and pillage.

Perhaps this is what makes these COP meetings in Durban, Copenhagen, Cancun, etc. such a magnificent waste of time: the more aggressive countries "just say no." No, we can't afford to close our coal plants; no, we feel no obligation; no, we'll be relatively unharmed by climate change; no, we don't care what the rest of the world thinks. In a word: *No.*

My suggestion: come to terms with the reality of the situation, i.e., cleantech solutions sit at the core of the economy of the 21st Century. The sooner we understand this and embrace it, the sooner we can grow our job base, and create a boom in real and sustainable prosperity.

Even Shell Oil says that solar will have overtaken oil by the year 2060. Yes, here's one of the world's wealthiest and most powerful opponents to clean energy that admits that the migration to renewable energy is inevitable. So why not now? Why not build a vibrant new economy while averting catastrophe?

The world is staring into the face of environmental degradation and resource depletion; it's a world facing the abyss of climate refugees, food and water shortages, and the other horrors brought on by our collective folly. This means, like it or not, that the development of cleantech and renewable energy more specifically is not just a nice idea; it's the only enterprise that has any real meaning in the 21st Century. The sooner we embrace this reality and build a new economy around cleantech, the sooner we can get on the road to true prosperity.

How much longer will it matter how cheaply you can manufacture ballpoint pens or I-pads or Cadillac Escalades? When drought has destroyed our farmland, and our industries and agribusinesses have poisoned our waters and skies, it will be too late to start thinking about clean energy, conservation, and energy efficiency.

Let's do it now. This won't hurt a bit.

## Iran and Syria: Using Vast Oil Profits — For What Purposes?

I'm anything but an expert on the Middle East, but this can't be good news: Iran and Syria signing a win-win agreement based on $3.6 billion in oil. When I see countries with criminally insane governments getting rich off oil, it engenders a range of thoughts and emotions – none of them positive. Obviously, I'm afraid of the implications in terms of human rights violations and the ever-growing prospect of nuclear war. But I'm also angry that oil is the de facto energy/transportation policy of my beloved nation.

How is it possible that our country borrows half a billion dollars a day and uses it to empower the world's most dangerous people? Does it make sense that we're driving up the national debt while actively eroding our security? Of course not. But as long as the oil companies essentially own our Congress, it's hard to imagine any change here.

I remember a talk that Ed Rendell, ex-governor of Pennsylvania, delivered to a packed house at the Renewable Energy Finance Forum, during which he spoke about the movement to alternative fuels and renewable energy, and then explained precisely why it's not happening. According to Rendell: "There are too many special interests arrayed against it. Over 90% of Democratic voters are in favor of Congress passing legislation that prioritizes clean energy. In fact, over 75% of Republican voters are in favor of the exact same thing. Clearly, the will of the American people is being frustrated by special interests."

"Together, we can do this," Rendell fairly bellowed in summary. "But we can't do it inside the Beltway. The lobbyists are raising campaign money for our senators and representatives in Washington seven days a week. It never stops. **It never stops.** There are fund-raisers happening literally every night. If change is going to happen, it needs to take place in hometown America. Your leaders have to hear it from you."

For what it's worth, I urge you to take Mr. Rendell up on his advice: tell your leaders that they need to be responsive to the will of the people, not their paymasters.

# Could the Price of Climate Change REALLY Be $60 Trillion?

/

What's the real imperative of the migration to renewable energy and cutting back our consumption of fossil fuels via efficiency and conservation? Might you say: Climate change?

We'll, that certainly one good answer. Of course, there are half a dozen others: dealing with peak oil, health issues, ocean acidification, the loss of biodiversity, human hostility, etc. When I'm interviewed on the subject and I encounter climate change deniers, I'm quick to change the subject. As I often say, "If you don't believe in climate change, that's fine, just pick another good reason to curb our addiction to fossil fuels; most of them have nothing to do with this dreaded subject whatsoever."

But having said all this, the build-up of greenhouse gases, which will eventually culminate in the melting of the arctic and the release of the methane beneath it, carries with it a fairly hefty price tag in terms of climate change per se, according to European researchers Gail Whiteman, from the school of management at Erasmus University in Rotterdam, Peter Wadhams, professor of ocean physics at the University of Cambridge, and Peter Hope, from the Judge Business School in Cambridge. In an article they published in the journal *Nature*, they try to piece together the cost of global climate change. Their total: $60 trillion.

Now wait a second. If the total world economy is estimated at $70 trillion annually, isn't this a very large number? Indeed it is.

Let's look at how they got there. Part of it is the valuation on human life that will be lost due to loss of homeland, flooding, starvation, dehydration, disease, etc. That's always amused me, btw, in some perverse way. Apparently, we feel fairly comfortable ascribing a certain dollar figure to a human life. Maybe our willingness to equate lives and dollars is why we're in this mess in the first place. It seems unlikely that Jesus, or Socrates, or Confucius would do that.

Be this as it may. Obviously, a lot of the rest of the damage is easier to quantify: the value of the real estate in low-lying areas like New York, Boston, Miami in the U.S. – and dozens of other huge cities around the world, that will cease to exist as the result of sea-level rise. Dollar figures like farmers' crop loss are equally easy to nail down with some level of precision.

In the U.S., we're unique in that many of us question the validity of anthropogenic global warming (AGW). And it's an issue that divides almost precisely across party lines, too: only 19% of Republicans agree with the 97% of climate scientists that AGW is a valid and potent threat to humankind.

That's interesting in and of itself, but consider this: none of this is lost on the business community. At the very same moment that the debate leaves the cocktail parties at the country clubs and the polo fields and enters the boardroom, everything changes. When the financial people have a voice, e.g., the insurance companies whose empires rise or fall according to the effects of climate change that are happening right this minute, e.g., extreme weather events, the unsupportable political opinions instantly disappear and science robustly takes over.

Check out the recent New York Times article that I just found from Googling "insurance companies climate change" – one of 20.5 million such hits, called "For Insurers, No Doubts on Climate Change." Evidently, the insurance industry, known for centuries for its mathematical precision, sees what's happening, and is acting accordingly. From the article:

*And the industry expects the situation will get worse. "Numerous studies assume a rise in summer drought periods in North America in the future and an increasing probability of severe cyclones relatively far north along the U.S. East Coast in the long term," said Peter Höppe, who heads Geo Risks Research at the reinsurance giant Munich Re. "The rise in sea level caused by climate change will further increase the risk of storm surge." Most insurers, including the reinsurance companies that bear much of the ultimate risk in the industry, have little time for the arguments heard in some right-wing circles that climate change isn't happening, and are quite comfortable with the scientific consensus that burning fossil fuels is the main culprit of global warming.*

*"Insurance is heavily dependent on scientific thought," Frank Nutter, president of the Reinsurance Association of America, told me last week.*

*"It is not as amenable to politicized scientific thought."*

We know that our fascination with cheap energy, stored in the Earth from the sun's rays over the last few billion years, is killing us, but it's our de facto energy policy nonetheless. What to make of the fact that we Americans are still dragging our heels and supporting our oil companies with continued subsidies and tax breaks, while letting them essentially run our government? In a word, it's pathetic.

# Is the Wind Energy Industry a Scam?

A friend sent me a long and scathing attack on the wind energy industry and writes: *"From friends in Connecticut—This has a lot of right wing "anti-green" rhetoric, but how much is factual?"*

Thanks very much. Good to hear from you again. Here are a few excerpts, along with my responses:

*There are many hidden truths about the world of wind turbines from the pollution and environmental damage caused in China by manufacturing bird choppers ... the countless numbers of birds that are killed each year.*

Yes, wind turbines kill birds – and bats. But a bird is 800 times more likely to be hit by a car, 1200 times more likely to fly into a plate-glass window, and many thousands of times more likely to be eaten by a house cat. Note also that the wind industry is working hard to improve in this arena.

*Wind energy is just a tax scam. Ben Lieberman, a senior policy analyst focusing on energy and environmental issues for the Heritage Foundation, is not surprised. He asks: "If wind power made sense, why would it need a government subsidy in the first place? It's a bubble which bursts as soon as the government subsidies end."*

The price of wind and the other main forms of renewable energy continue to fall each year, and it's very clear to everyone who is honestly trying to make sense of the issue that subsidies will not be required much longer. As it is, the subsidies for wind are continually coming and going — unlike the subsidies bestowed to the oil companies, which have been in place for 90 years, and persist in making the wealthiest industry on Earth even wealthier – all at tax-payers' expense. And not to get into character assassination, but the Heritage Foundation is hardly a bastion of integrity. If you read a few articles on them, you'll see why I think you should feel much more comfortable taking moral direction from the neoNazis or the KKK.

*Like solar panels, windmills produce less energy before they break down than the energy it took to make them.*

*That's the part liberals forget: making windmills and solar panels takes energy, energy from coal, oil, and diesel, energy that extracts and refines raw materials, energy that transports those materials to where they will be re-shaped into finished goods,*

*energy to manufacture those goods. More energy than those finished windmills and solar panels will ever produce.*

One could argue that there is a grain of truth in the "right-wing rhetoric" above (to use your term), but not in this one; it's completely false. Google: "EROI wind" (energy return on investment."

I leave you with a link to Energy Fact Check, a really good — and honest — source for the truth on the subject. Thanks again for writing.

# American Council on Renewable Energy Blends Passion with a Zen-like Demeanor

A few months ago I interviewed Dennis McGinn, the current president of the American Council on Renewable Energy (ACORE) for my third book ("Renewable Energy – Following the Money"). I've also met his predecessor in that post, Micheal Eckhart, several times at various conferences.

I deeply admire both these folks, perhaps mostly for the comportment with which they approach the challenge. It blends a core passion with a calm levelheadedness that I think is important in an arena that invites such controversy. When I occasionally run into idiots who attack me and renewable energy as some sort of anti-capitalist plot whose only economic viability is feeding off the government teat, I try to smile and lay out the facts. But I can feel my blood pressure surge every time I go through this exercise. What if that were my 60-hour/week job? I wonder how long I could keep rising to the occasion without losing my temper.

In any case, Mike Eckhart may be the all-time champ at taking deep breaths at laying all this out so calmly that it's as soothing as the bed-time story that your father told you 500 times to ease you off to sleep.

His position is that we're about 40 years into a 100-year migration to clean energy. He starts us off in 1970 when the Clean Air Act was passed and the EPA was formed, then goes on to the Clean Water Act in 1972, the Oil Shock in 1973 that put energy and the environment on the table, the Iranian Revolution and the second doubling of oil prices, the stagflation/inflation in the 1980s. He continues on to detail the "valley of death" for renewables, which was mitigated for a time by restructuring, deregulation, and the production tax credit. At this point, wind energy was owned by big tax-paying companies, just as the new independent power industry was owned by the utilities.

Next, he explains how Europe and Japan moved into renewable energy in the late 90s, while the U.S. argued about utility restructuring. The G.W. Bush administration's national energy plan pushed oil, gas and coal, and the World Energy Council was formed to thwart the U.S. focus on fossil fuels. So here we are today, trying to create a level playing field, hoping to extend the initial incentives, and watching China knock the cover off the ball. Again, we're only 40 years through a 100-year process.

For what it's worth, I agree. Even Shell Oil says that by 2060, all the Earth's energy will be solar, so perhaps this isn't all that controversial. And that would be completely true if it weren't for a few good questions:

- How much damage will we do to human health and our natural environment in the process? and

- Who's going to make a buck as we move through time here?

The answer is that the oil companies don't care about question #1 as long as they're the answer to question #2. That's what makes all this interesting — and what renders me utterly incapable of discussing the subject dispassionately. People who think like that are profoundly morally defective. It's hard to take this lying down.

# Coal Industry Will Not Go Gentle Into That Good Night

In a recent article from SmartGridNews, we see what anyone could have predicted from the incumbent industries in response to U.S. President Obama's speech on climate policy: *instant attack*, including the threat of litigation. Of course, the concept that the content of any speech will translate directly and quickly into action that negatively affects a powerful interest is really a fantasy.

From the article:

*Jo Ann Emerson, CEO of the National Rural Electric Cooperative Association (NRECA), was having none of it: "Electric cooperatives oppose President Obama's proposal to use the Clean Air Act to reduce carbon dioxide emissions from power plants. America's rural communities depend on coal-fired generation for affordable electric power and would be disproportionately penalized by this scheme." NRECA pledged to fight Obama's strategy "at the agency level and in the courts if necessary."*

and...

*John Pippy, CEO of the Pennsylvania Coal Alliance, defended the coal industry's record and efforts to reduce pollution and said in a news release that the president's plan is "shortsighted and destructive to the nation's fragile economic recovery." He added, "There are tens of thousands of good-paying jobs at stake here."*

Yes, John, there are tens of thousands of good-paying jobs at stake, but there are also seven billion people with lungs, and an entire biosphere threatened by climate change, ocean acidification, loss of bio-diversity, etc.

## Hope, Activism, and Climate Change

2GreenEnergy supporter Cameron Atwood sent me an incredible, wide-ranging article by political activist Rebecca Solnit. Its theme is critically important to people trying to making sense of our modern world – and especially to those of us trying to change it for the better. Simply put: we all make a difference, and we honestly have no idea of the magnitude of the impact we're making: it's just too early to know. I urge you to treat yourself to this short, readable masterpiece.

When you think about it, the world is an unimaginably different place than it was just a few decades ago. In terms of the things I follow most closely, e.g., climate change, I note that in 2003 there was essentially no public recognition for the phenomenon itself, and certainly no swelling of mainstream consciousness that we had a duty to change our ways of energy generation and consumption accordingly. Yet only 10 years later, we have enormous numbers of people blocking the construction of tar sands pipelines, and taking all manner of other actions all over the globe. True, not all are risking arrest as they assert their convictions, but that's really not what it takes anyway, as a few of the most active and visible people have enormous amounts of leverage.

Solnit writes: "Things change. And people sometimes have the power to make that happen, if and when they come together and act (and occasionally act alone, as did writers Rachel Carson and Harriet Beecher Stowe — or Mohammed Bouazizi, the young man whose suicide triggered the Arab Spring)."

And it's not all about "activism"; we have many credible business people talking about Copenhagen's becoming a carbon-neutral city by 2025, and we see the world's biggest financial institutions: Credit Suisse, Citigroup, Deutsche Bank, etc., investing literally trillions of dollars into energy efficiency and clean energy solutions. That was completely unthinkable 10 years ago.

We tend to think of the future as an extension of the past, yet this is very rarely the case, and it's especially unlikely in the 21st Century. Or, as George Will (hardly a progressive visionary) told me at last year's reunion of our alma mater, "the future always looks like the past – until it looks like something completely different."

In fact, the most striking aspect of Solnit's work of art here is a kind of intellectual humility that defines good thinking today. Our position needs to be: we really don't know how all this is going to turn out. Optimists think everything will be fine; pessimists don't see a way out. Solnit concludes: "Will we get (there)? I don't know. Neither do you."

## Does Corporate Sustainability Pay for Itself?

There were some very thought-provoking presentations at the quarterly "Sustainability Partners Conference" at UCLA yesterday. At issue is a central question: does sustainability pay for itself? I.e., do companies that have vigorously and sincerely woven sustainability in their corporate DNA experience enhanced profit as a result? The answer one takes away from these presentations is that the answer is generally Yes.

But I'm not convinced. Obviously, if you're Patagonia, you've tapped into a market segment that cares about this stuff and will pay more for a product, clothing in this case, that gets great marks in terms of carbon footprint, free trade, etc. The program included a talk by a spokesperson of Dr. Bronner's Magical Soap, a product that came of age in the 1960s, and has done very well to maintain a customer base that embraces all the good things that came along in that era: a sense of caring, community, eco-friendliness, getting back to nature, etc. Will this (small) segment pay more for soap that comes from organic farms where all workers are paid a living wage, where the product itself contains no terrible chemicals? Of course it will. Dr. Bronner's revenues are $60 million, and it's not really surprising that the company can maintain or even expand that base, though we need to keep in mind that, by comparison, Dial Soap just sold for $2.9 billion.

But what if you're Mattel? A spokesperson from this toy behemoth ($7.5 billion in revenues) spoke next; she did a great talk, and was quite candid with her stories, for example, how Green Peace was all over them in a PR nightmare lasting several months when it was discovered that some of their packaging came from clear-cutting the rainforests in Indonesia. Granted, it's of some value (probably *considerable* value) to avoid these public relations disasters. But here are products that are picked out by boys and girls ages 3 – 12 who (generally) don't grok LCAs (lifecycle analyses) and all that other good stuff.

Of course, when any company gets serious about sustainability, it finds areas where it can save cold hard cash that has simply been being wasted. But it also encounters significant costs. I find it very hard to believe that Mattel can point to increased net profits associated with sustainability. The spokesperson was cheerful and bright, obviously very happy to be a driving force in her company's quest to do the right thing, but she sidestepped this issue.

Last week, the world received a wake-up call from Bangladesh re: the apparel industry. We learned what we should have known all along: the fashion brands are on a ravenous nonstop, planet-wide hunt for the least cost places to manufacture product that meets whatever quality standard it feels it must maintain. Up until now, it has had (and we can only hope this is changing) sparse concern for child labor, worker safety, living wage, decent hours, humane conditions, etc.

For what it's worth, I deeply sympathize with the woman from Mattel and how difficult all this is. The company sells 8000 different toys, and 80% of them are new every year. It has 1500 quality control people who test these, largely looking for safety issues, but they can't test every toy, and they certainly can't get 100% transparency on 100% of these suppliers, as some of these chains are three and four layers deep. (This, btw, is why it took the Europeans so long to learn that they were eating horsemeat: the supply chain for meat products on the Continent is incredibly convoluted; product passes through dozens of different hands before it's sold to the consumer.)

I see a day coming where CEOs will need to sign off on sustainability statements the same way they sign off on financial reporting today. CEOs weren't thrilled when they realized they could go to jail if their financial reporting was incorrect; I doubt they're going to fall in love with another zone of worry, and I'm sure we'll have attorneys fighting this concept for a very long time to come. But I don't see a way around this if we really want to put an end to collapsing factories and clear-cutting rainforests.

If sustainability actually generates more profit, that's fine. But if it doesn't, and it turns out to be a cost of doing business, that's fine too.

## We Want Clean Energy, But Getting Congress To Act Is Tough

I occasionally like to write something purely for the 43% of 2GreenEnergy readers who reside outside the United States and may have difficulty understanding how profoundly broken our legal and political processes are here, or who may think I'm exaggerating when I discuss our government's flagrant disregard for the clearly expressed will of the people it ostensibly represents. Previously I wrote:

*Colorado Governor Bill Ritter told a packed house at the <u>Renewable Energy Finance Forum</u> a few weeks ago the following story… The University of Colorado at Boulder recently completed a survey of many thousands of residents from around the state, in which participants provided their viewpoints on a myriad of energy-related issues. Among other things, the study showed that an overwhelming majority favored a bill on the floor of Congress that would place a tax on carbon and create financial incentive for businesses and households to reduce their carbon footprints. To Ritter's astonishment, one of the senators from his state, under pressure from special interests, went back to Congress and voted against the bill that his constituents had so clearly favored.*

Early today, we saw, albeit on another subject, an even more blatant example of the same concept, concerning the issue of reformation of our gun control laws, which I bring up not to take sides, but to amplify my point. According to recent polls, almost exactly 90% of Americans favor more aggressive gun control, and one might have expected this to translate into robust discussion, leading to swift action. Wrong. It took an amazing amount of work to have the subject broached in Congress, and, a few hours ago, our Senate voted it down, under pressure from a super-powerful lobby organization (our National Rifle Association)—the tool of the enormously profitable gun/ammo manufacturing industry.

My point is simply this: If our Senate, yielding to the pressure of Big Money, can spurn the demands of a full 90% of the American people, how surprised can we be that we can't get traction around clean energy and transportation? Comments from readers outside the U.S. often reveal that they view what's happening here with a mixture of pity and contempt; it's really not hard to see why.

# We All Wield Tremendous Power to Restore Environmental Justice

I wrote a post recently in which I mentioned the Black Swan effect, i.e., the tendency of human beings to underestimate the importance and frequency of unforeseeable events in the future. This concept, popularized by Nassim Taleb in his 2007 masterpiece, has implications in many different arenas of human activity, principally economics/investments, where we tend to make long-term bets with little appreciation of the huge potential impact of the unanticipated and unknowable.

Part and parcel of all this is the effect that one person can have on human civilization as a whole. Needless to say, there have been many such examples throughout history.

The classic example of this in the recent past was the publication, about a hundred fifty years ago, of Harriet Beecher Stowe's Uncle Tom's Cabin. Of course, Northerners in the middle part of the 19th Century had a general understanding that slavery was an evil and brutal empire, but the incredible popularity of Stowe's book (1852) provided a ferociously powerful galvanizing effect upon the many millions of people living in those states, driving them to a state of fury that such an institution should be allowed to exist in a civilized society. Eleven years (and many millions of war casualties) later the Emancipation Proclamation became law, two years after which the Thirteenth Amendment permanently enshrined this into the U.S. Constitution.

Far more recently we've seen similar acts of individual triumph and bravery that served to catalyze movements no one could have possibly foreseen, some of which define our world of today, e.g., the man who defied the Chinese tanks at Tienanmen Square, and the young fellow who lighted himself on fire, spawning the Arab Spring.

I bring this up because the other day marked the 43rd anniversary of the law in the United States that banned the use of the chemical DDT. As we all know, this was the direct result of Rachel Carson's book Silent Spring, published in 1963. Remarkably, up until that point, Western culture had never seriously questioned the notion that the world around us was our slave, and that we could mistreat it with complete impunity, as no physical means existed by which it could cease to treat its master with love and respect. We of European heritage had incorrectly assumed that there was no real and lasting harm we could inflict upon the natural order of things by way of our implementation of even the most toxic of chemical poisons, the mass destruction of natural resources, etc.

One book, with one author, changed that forever. 50+ years after the fact, it's hard to put the magnitude of this paradigm shift into perspective. It's really akin to the Copernican Revolution 500 years ago, or the onset of the Western Enlightenment about 400 years ago where science began to replace superstition: suddenly things started to make sense.

Amazingly, there are still a few people alive today who hold close to that notion that humankind has free rein to do anything it wants here on Earth without regard for the effects its actions have on the ecosystems around us. Fortunately, such people form a small and ever-diminishing minority at this point; in just that half a century, the world has almost completely come to understand that everything we do has a cascading effect on the environment around us, and that all of us bear responsibilities according.

I believe that stories of individuals who changed the world forever are good messages for us all to carry around with ourselves in our daily lives. Never forget that you and I, and all the people around us, can make a difference of untold proportion in the outcome of our civilization.

## Quibbling on the Definition of "Sustainability" — And Other Words

The other day, I wrote a comment on an article that dealt with the sustainability of dog ownership, in response to which someone pointed out: *I guess it depends on how you define "sustainability."*

True, it may be hard, or even impossible, to work out a precise definition of "sustainable" that applies in all cases. In fact, a number of people have suggested that we stop using the term altogether simply because it means so many different things in various contexts.

I totally disagree with this latter idea.

No better word in the English language exists to communicate the idea here, though, obviously, if you want to pick nits on the subject, you won't get anywhere at all. We can all agree that sustainable processes are those that, a) can be continued indefinitely though time, b) result in a minimum of toxic byproducts, c) don't abuse or exploit members of the human race, d) don't pose a constant drain on finite natural resources without a way to replenish them and, e) don't cause unacceptable amounts of damage elsewhere in the ecosystem.

I just wrote this off the top of my head, and I'm sure there are more complete, elegant, and unassailable ways of expressing the idea. In fact, it may sound like a lot of words for such a simple concept, but consider an example. What if I told you that I had a way to raise and catch wild tuna that was minimally polluting and left the tuna population essentially unchanged? You might say that this was by definition "sustainable," until I admitted that it would wipe out 90% of the seal population in a matter of a few decades, or that it posed incredible safety risks to fishermen, at which you'd be forced to admit that my plan is not really "sustainable" in any meaningful way.

Again, not to be cavalier, but I think the *intention of the term*, as it's commonly used by thoughtful people who honestly care about the subject, is completely clear.

This provides an opportunity for a segue: There happens to be an interesting coincidence happening in the U.S. right this moment surrounding this concept of the "intention of the term." Readers outside the country may be unaware that our Supreme Court has agreed to re-consider the constitutionality of the Affordable Care Act ("Obamacare"), based on the fact that the actual words in the law may result in an unacceptable burden on the states vs. the federal government–even though it is 100% clear that this was a simple error, i.e., the lawmakers' mistaken choice of words; it was certainly not part of the intention of the law.

Now you might be one of the people (like me) everywhere who say, "Well, if you're so sure that the authors of the law intended X, why don't you simply ask them? Wouldn't that put an end to any doubt that might exist in anyone's mind? This was just two years ago in 2012; just ask them to clarify what they meant. It's not like you're trying to interview the people who wrote the Bible—or even the Constitution itself. Just walk across the street (First Street Northeast in Washington, DC) and *ask them*.

Most people interpret the Constitution this way (above), though not all. For example, Antonin Scalia, who I believe played a pivotal role in the decision to re-hear the case, is what is called a "textualist." This means that to him, the intention of the law doesn't matter in the slightest; the only thing that counts is the precise words that appear in the law themselves.

This strikes me as extremely backward; it sounds like some relic of jurisprudence from before Hammurabi's time. Yes, it's given the academically appealing name "textualism," but it seems more like "obstructionism" or "regressivism," or some other word that means "a doctrine that facilitates attempts to block civilization's efforts to make itself more civilized."

In any case, we'll see what happens here.

In the meanwhile, for what it's worth, I'm "thumbs up" on the word "sustainable."

# Humankind's Chances for a "Soft Landing" Re: the Environment

Here's another piece of my conversation with a reader on the subject of government's role vis-à-vis bringing about positive change re: the deteriorating conditions surrounding our environment: climate disruption, ocean acidification, increasing levels of toxicity, loss of biodiversity, etc.

I had previously offered her a laundry list of actions that I would take in this arena if I suddenly found myself promoted to "king of the world."

The reader comments in return: *I can't dispute any of your points. Everything you mentioned (should be put into place). My problem is that the more government takes responsibility, the more we lose.*

You really nailed a key issue, i.e., corruption and inefficiency in government. Some days I wake up wondering how this civilization can possibly make the changes that are required for its survival on this planet. The outlook isn't exactly brilliant, to paraphrase the great poem.

Here's a brief discussion of the three major forces at play:

*Government.* Again, you have a very strong point here. We all talk about the stalemate in Washington, i.e., that virtually everyone there bears the responsibility to sabotage progress of any type if it comes from the other side of the aisle. As sickening as that may be, that's the tip of the iceberg. Our 435 U.S. Representatives are elected on two-year cycles, and the process of leading us out of this mess is a long-term (several-decade-long) endeavor. Any "representative" who takes on an issue that doesn't enhance the financial position of the masses in his district will soon be an "ex-representative." Not only is he turning off his voters, he's handing his opponents a lethally effective set of tools to disgrace and thus remove him.

And even that's just the beginning; it gets far worse. Hoping for progress from government presumes that these "leaders" actually care about the wellbeing of the people they "serve," where, in fact, nothing could be further from the truth. Those who believe they have a friend in Washington (unless it's a paid friend) are credulous in the extreme. Politicians are elected with enormous sums of dark money, super-PACs, etc. that demand and receive huge favors in return. And how likely is it that these favors will involve laws/regulations/incentives that might slow the onslaught of destruction against the environment? Zero.

The same calculus applies at different levels and in different ways to the rest of the federal government, as well as most of state and local, except in certain specific regions that happen to have a disproportionately high number of well-educated people. (If you want an interesting exercise, compare a map of the red and blue states to the percentage of college graduates in those states.)

In any case, you're right here: hoping for effective, competent, efficient, and honest leadership from government is akin to hoping that my dog (pictured above) will learn to speak French. I love him, but he hasn't shown much aptitude so far.

*The Private Sector.* Similarly, Big Oil spends hundreds of millions of dollars per year in PR campaigns to convince the common idiot American voter that climate change is a hoax/fraud, that U.S. interests are best served by fossil fuels, that taking action to respect the environment will damage the economy, and that such action is meaningless folly—the dreams of idealistic hippies whose grasp of the basic math is so weak that they lack the capacity to understand the problem. Big Money (including Big Oil) also owns the media. 95% of every word you read in print or see in electronic media comes from a handful (I believe it's five or six) mega-news organizations, whose messages to these sheep/voters are extremely tightly controlled. This makes it quite difficult for Americans, even if they are so inspired, to learn enough about the subject to join the rest of the world in terms of an understanding of the limits of industry, population growth, and shortages of energy, water, and food.

Having said that, a great number of private sector organizations really ARE making some very important contributions in terms of social responsibility. Some have experienced a lucky coincidence, and have found that they're actually saving money by eliminating waste. Others have a customer base that is willing to pay extra for eco-friendly products, e.g., Patagonia and Whole Foods. These, however, constitute a very small minority of corporate interests. Those that really deserve our praise are the entities whose CSR (corporate social responsibility) programs represent a net loss in profit, but are in place because their stake-holders are people of true decency and character. I hope you'll join me in applauding every single one of them.

*The People.* As I've written dozens of times, there are more than 200,000 groups on Earth whose missions are social and environmental justice. Some are quite small, (e.g., this one–the 2GreenEnergy subscriber/regular visitor base, which is measured in tens of thousands. Other are huge (e.g., The Sierra Club, 350.org, the Natural Resources Defense Council (NRDC) – each with many millions of members, etc.). In any case, I think anyone, regardless of his politics, needs to admit that this represents an enormous amount of horsepower—and it's growing by the day.

But will it be sufficient to put enough pressure on the workings of the world to make a difference while there is still time? I don't know. It's too soon to tell.

In fact, when I speak in public on the subject, I often encounter people in the Q&A sessions that follow who claim that humankind is screwed, that we're looking into the abyss of the Sixth Extinction (a reference to the eponymous best-seller), etc. I smile and say, "OK, fair enough. You're a pessimist. I totally understand that, and I'll wager that you're joined in this room by a considerable percentage of the audience—perhaps half, or even more." I ask for a show of hands, which usually validates that I'm right. I then make some joke, like, "We better break out the good wine NOW, while there's still time to savor its rich bouquet and complex character." But then I get serious again, and explain, "Have you ever had the thought that optimists and pessimists, paradoxically, share something in common? They both think they know how this is going to come out. You should know that I spend most of my waking hours studying this subject, and I have to tell you, honest to God, I believe it's too early to tell. So, to the question: How is this going to come out? I need to confess: I don't know. And with all due respect, neither do you."

# Part Five: Conclusion

I hope I've succeeded in leaving readers with the same kind of "rational exuberance" that I happen to have here. If the pricing for clean energy in all its many forms suggested that fossil fuels would remain the far cheaper alternative for the indefinite future, I'd grant that the pragmatists among us should pack our bags, buy stock in ExxonMobil, and head for the mountains. I say this, of course, because we need to live with the fact that market economics is the only factor that can be trusted to mean anything in the world today.

But that's the precise problem facing the fossil fuel boys, and it's an insurmountable one: there is no power on Earth (no amount of cash, no buying politicians, no exploiting weaker nations and their powerless people, no passing laws to force our military to stay away from alternative fuels, etc.) that can be used to maintain the energy status quo in an environment when renewable energy solutions are rapidly becoming so financially attractive.

The point that I made in the last couple of chapters in Part Two is that, on top of this, there is bound to be a beneficial effect from changing consumer sensibilities vis-à-vis our health and our environment. I hope I made the case that even the dimmest bulbs among us are starting to realize that they've been lied to, and thus

Big Energy's enormous propaganda machine is in the process of grinding to a halt.

As usual, I'll close by thanking you for reading my book, and, more to the point, I'll thank you for being among that small but ever-growing number of people who honestly care about stuff like this.

I remain anxious to speak with anyone who would like to take the discussion forward from here, and I can be reached through my website: 2GreenEnergy.com.

# Appendix - Global Warming

Global warming is the process by which certain gases in the atmosphere - known as greenhouse gases trap energy from the sun.

The main mechanism by which this happens is sunlight passing through the Earth's atmosphere and heating up surfaces, clouds, dust etc. As these get hot, they re-radiate light in the infrared part of the spectrum. Greenhouse gases in the atmosphere such as water, $CO_2$, nitrous oxide, chlorofluorocarbons methane, etc. absorb and block a proportion of the infrared light thus produced, rather like the glass in a greenhouse, so making it harder for Earth to get rid of heat by radiation.

As a consequence, the temperature of the Earth's surface is higher than it would be without these gases in the atmosphere. When greenhouse gases increase, the Earth's surface gets hotter until it warms enough to radiate sufficient heat to balance incoming sunshine. As the Earth is large, a great deal of energy is required to raise its temperature, so a rapid change in greenhouse gases will result in a relatively slow rise in temperature which will continue for a long time before solar heat received is once again in balance with infrared heat given out.

There are two parts to the "greenhouse effect," the cause of global warming.

## The Natural Greenhouse Effect

Certain gases naturally occurring in the atmosphere trap heat from the sun. Primarily, these are carbon dioxide ($CO_2$), water, methane and nitrous oxide ($NOx$). Naturally occurring concentrations of these gases keep the average temperature of the Earth's surface at around 15C rather than the -18C that would occur in their absence. The natural greenhouse effect is therefore essential to keeping the Earth in suitable condition for its present abundant life.

Of these gases, water vapor provides the biggest contribution to the greenhouse effect, but cycles in and out of the atmosphere quickly before condensing out as rain or snow. $CO_2$ is the second largest contributor and, on the other hand, generally remains in the atmosphere for many years, so any change in $CO_2$ levels will tend to be persistent and have a long-term effect on climate. The natural greenhouse effect would tend to keep the Earth's overall average temperature relatively stable most of the time, though with periodic disturbances caused by factors such as volcanos, large meteorite impact, evolution of new species (such as the period in which flowering plants evolved), and natural cycles such as the gradual movement of the geographical poles, and changes in ocean currents. These account for ice ages, periods where the Earth had very little ice, and for a number of comparatively short-term climate changes.

## The Manmade Greenhouse Effect

For thousands of years, man has been cutting down forests, disturbing natural ecosystems, and burning fossil fuels. There is for example, evidence of coal mining and use in Roman Britain, and of even more ancient burning of both coal and pitch in various locations. Through these kinds of activities, man has for all this time been disturbing the naturally occurring concentrations of greenhouse gases, and so at least potentially contributing to climate change by altering atmospheric levels of $CO_2$.

Some commentators believe that the Little Ice Age might have been aggravated by the Black Death of the 1340's in which millions of people throughout Europe and Asia died, causing much of the farmland to revert to forest. The Little Ice Age was a period from around 1500 to 1800, during which temperatures were on the order of 1C lower than before or immediately after.

Other commentators believe that human activity would only have provided a small signal at that time, which would have been damped out by the ocean, and could not have had a significant effect on the Little Ice Age. Although not proven beyond doubt, this evidence would at least suggest anecdotally that when the $CO_2$ level in the atmosphere changes, the full effects might take centuries to work through.

Since 1800, there has been a massive increase in global human population together with a huge rise in industrial production and energy use. Of the greenhouse gases, human activity has changed $CO_2$ concentrations the most. Human impacts on water vapor are important in a local context: overgrazing/deforestation can cause local desertification, however, human effects are largely washed out at the global scale by the hydrological cycle.

By comparison, other greenhouse gases including those previously mentioned, as well as ozone and halo-carbons, make up a much smaller part of the total effect; some are much more powerful greenhouse gases than $CO_2$, but are present in concentrations 1000 to 1,000,000 times lower in the atmosphere.

$CO_2$ has been directly measured in Hawaii since 1958, and inferred indirectly from various sources for earlier periods (such as gas bubbles trapped in ice cores, etc.). It is believed that $CO_2$ levels have risen from around 270 parts per million at the start of the industrial revolution to just over 400 parts per million in 2014. The global average temperature is now believed to be around 1C higher than in the 1860's, with most scientists believing that most or all of the rise is a result of human activity.

As solar heat input is currently greater than infra-red output, an imbalance caused by the blocking effects of additional greenhouse gases in the atmosphere arising from human activity, the Earth can be expected to continue warming for some time; this will happen even in the absence of further rises in greenhouse gas concentration. Warming will continue until the Earth gets hot enough to send out enough infrared heat through the blanket of greenhouse gases to balance solar heat input.

## Some Basis Physics on the Subject

All surfaces at temperatures above absolute zero emit radiation the wavelength of which is determined primarily by temperature. The energy content of emitted radiation rises in proportional to the 4th power of temperature on the absolute (Kelvin) scale. In the case of the Earth, emission occurs in the infrared part of the spectrum, while for the sun, with its much higher surface temperature, emission is largely in the visible part of the spectrum. The addition of human induced $CO_2$ and other greenhouse gases stops some infrared light leaving the atmosphere, and so causes a net input of energy into the Earth's surface. As mentioned above, this will stop only when hotter conditions increase infrared production sufficiently to produce a new balance. Due to the very large thermal mass of the Earth's surface, its atmosphere, and oceans, a small net energy input per square meter can take a long time to increase temperature, so that heat input and output can be out of balance for a extended periods. For this reason, a temperature rise caused by greenhouse gases already in the atmosphere is likely to continue for at least 100 years.

Yet this physical form of inertia is not the only inertia in the system. Built infrastructure and political inertia discussed below are of equal or greater importance, as they prevent any rapid reduction of human induced greenhouse gas production. In practice, we are as yet nowhere near to stopping the rise in manmade greenhouse gas in the atmosphere, the production of which is actually currently accelerating. As a result, not only can the Earth be expected to keep warming for 100 years or more, but the rate of change can be expected to increase significantly.

## Built Infrastructure Inertia

Every power station, vehicle, factory, road, cement plant, coalmine, etc. is built and designed to last a certain amount of time, normally between 10 and 100 years. This being the case, most of the built infrastructure, as well as much that has been planned and approved for construction will in all probability continue to pump greenhouse gases into the atmosphere for most or all of its design life. Decisions already made, and to which mankind is already committed, will almost certainly continue to increase greenhouse gas emissions for the next 20 years, and quite possibly beyond that. Even with serious efforts to curb greenhouse gas emissions, it is likely that emissions will continue to rise but at a slower rate than would otherwise have been the case. As the atmosphere is already receiving $CO_2$ significantly faster than it can get rid of it, not only will $CO_2$ levels rise, they will do so at an increasing rate, most likely for several more decades, so continuing to accelerate climate change.

# Political Inertia

Political systems of any kind, democratic or authoritarian, tend to take a considerable time to make decisions, and are not always able to achieve the results desired from any legislation passed. Given that in the democratic parts of the world, political parties are elected every few years, it is very difficult for any politician to make and carry through a politically unpopular decision. Scientific evidence suggests that human greenhouse gas emissions need to not just stabilize, but drop by 60% to 80% over the next 25 to 30 years in order to keep $CO_2$ concentrations below 500 parts per million. It is thought that by preventing a larger rise, and then reducing atmospheric $CO_2$ concentration in the following period, that some of the more serious consequences of global warming might be avoided. For example, that major melting of the Greenland and Antarctic ice might be avoided. One way to achieve such a reduction would be to introduce rationing of energy and everything dependent on it for production, including food and water. However, it would most likely prove politically impossible to maintain such a general form of rationing in peace time, as any party making such a commitment would find itself thrown out at the next election.

Likewise, political parties are dependent on donations and taxes directly or indirectly coming from the business community, thus limiting the scope for decisions adversely affecting the business interests of these organizations. Political decisions unpopular with such organizations, such as increased regulation or taxation are therefore likely to have a serious impact on the financial stability of political parties, and on national economies. Additionally, in a global market, companies are constantly seeking out more favorable locations. As a result of this, even if a government or governments decided to ration greenhouse gas emissions, as happens in Europe, many companies will simply move energy intensive operations to less regulated developing countries such as India and China and so bypass European regulation. This being the case, only a global treaty including *all* the major economic players stands any chance of success. Even with an ever increasing scientific consensus, there remain politicians who deny the existence of manmade global warming, or who underplay its importance. This may be from ignorance, or could be for political / economic gain. Many politicians owe their political success to donations from the fossil fuel industry or other major greenhouse gas producers, or are elected by constituents dependent on these industries for their jobs. For all these reasons, together with organizational problems such as delays in the planning process, change is slow. This is compounded by the general reluctance of people to actively sort out problems until they become too painful or inconvenient to ignore, and a widespread tendency to disregard/disobey any law which is inconvenient, expensive, or otherwise contentious. In practice, this makes the process of limiting the rise in greenhouse gases very challenging, especially and in the timeframe required to limit the risk of major climate change, which is a task requiring a huge and long-lasting global effort.

## Global Dimming

As well as producing $CO_2$, combustion of fossil fuels has resulted in the emission of sulphate aerosols and particulate pollution. These emissions affect the amount of light reaching the Earth's surface, and are considered to be offsetting some of the greenhouse warming associated with $CO_2$. Until the late 1990's, dimming was increasing, but in the last 10 years, measures taken to reduce these pollutants in particular in Europe and America have begun to reduce the effect. Unlike $CO_2$, sulfur and particulates have a short period of residency in the atmosphere. Even so, some estimates put the cooling effect associated with dimming at 50% of the warming associated with $CO_2$. In other words, without these pollutants, the heating effect of global warming might have been twice as great. The range of estimates of this cooling effect vary over a four-fold range, meaning that by cleaning up remaining sulphur and particulates, global temperatures might rise by something of the order of 0.2 to 0.8C. In other words, there has been a hidden warming potential of 0.2 to 0.8C so that the greenhouse effect will inevitably be added to further as these pollutants decrease.

Taking in the known existing temperature rise of around 0.75C, the delayed warming effect which will occur before equilibrium is re-established of possibly around 1C, and the concealed effect of warming masked by dimming of around 0.2 to 0.8C, the likely warming associated with human activity as will be seen in 2100 compared to the pre-industrial period, without further increase in atmospheric $CO_2$ but with removal of anthropogenic sulphur and particulates is approximately 1.9 to 2.6C. In fact, allowing for almost certain continuing $CO_2$ rises over the next 30 years or so, temperatures by 2100 are likely to rise by rather more than the 1.9 to 2.6C indicated above.

## Positive Signs

In recent years, there has been a substantial growth in the amount of energy derived from renewable sources such as solar power, solar heat, wind power, biomass, and the use of geothermal resources.

In the 10-year period from 2003 to 2012, cumulative solar PV capacity increased by 3,600% with the cost of solar generated power declining rapidly so that "merchant solar" contracts are now being signed in some markets, such as Chile, in which a solar power plant is built to sell power into the spot market without any form of government incentive. Costs continue to decline and the rate of global solar installation continues to rise.

Overall, in 2012, renewables formed over half of net new generation capacity with the quantity installed each year continuing to rise both in absolute terms, and as a percentage of net new capacity.

In the same 10-year period, cumulative wind capacity has increased by seven-fold with the average capacity factor of wind turbines also improving significantly over the period so that for each MW installed, more megawatt hours are generated due to longer turbine blades, higher hub height, and other technical improvements.

There is still a long road to travel, but with further technological improvements, "learning curve" whereby technologies become less expensive with increased volume, and other reductions in capital, O & M, administrative, (permitting, etc.), and financing costs arising from maturing renewable technologies, and some measure of political leadership, there is every reason to believe that renewable energy sources will supply an increasing proportion of total demand, and that within a few decades, the amount of fossil fuels consumed will begin to decline.

## The Warming Pause

While the vast majority of climate scientists believe that the theory of anthropomorphic climate change arising from the emission of greenhouse gas is proven, there is a stubborn rump of denial from a few individuals who insist that climate change is a natural phenomenon over which human activity has little or no influence. Generally, these people do not deny that our climate changes, or the basic theory of how greenhouse gases work, rather they point to natural variations in currents, the jet stream, solar output, sun spots, and the procession of the Earth by which the position of the poles vary cyclically, and assert that variations in these natural cycles rather than human activity are responsible for climate change. They also further assert that the climate is no longer warming and has not been for the last 15 years.

In some cases, denialists will acknowledge that human influence on local climate exists. They have no problem acknowledging local effects arising from humans causing changes in vegetation and humidity, such as when forest is replaced with crops, or through the "urban heat island" effect through changes in humidity, albedo and wind speeds. In fact, one of their arguments against manmade global climate change is that meteorological station readings are most likely to be made in areas with substantial human influence where local warming is measured creating the illusion of global warming; they're saying that global warming is an illusion caused by observational bias. Of course, serious climate scientists are well aware of these local influences, and make every effort to exclude or correct for them.

In regards to the more serious point about the alleged pause in warming, it is broadly true that average temperatures as measured on land in inhabited areas have not changed very much in the last 15 years. The denialists fail to mention two important exceptions.

*Temperature changes at high latitudes*

I urge readers to examine the work of the Danish Meteorological Institute (DMI) Arctic Air Temperatures and the Goddard Institute of Space Science (GISS) Arctic Surface Temperature Anomalies, and Implications for Arctic Warming.

Both of the above sources clearly show a rising trend in arctic temperatures, which if anything appear to have accelerated over the last 15 years – as is also shown by the declining trend in arctic sea ice area in successive summers. Further information, is available from The National Snow and Ice Data Centre.

*Transfer of heat to the deep oceans*

There are a number of cyclical processes in ocean and atmospheric circulation. Rather than there being a real pause in the net flow of heat into the Earth's atmosphere from the sun, it is believed that much of the excess heat has been transferred from the air to the oceans, stabilizing atmospheric temperatures in temperate latitudes at the cost of faster temperature rises in the sea.

According to an article in Scientific American, Aug 22, 2014, the pause in warming is explained by a net flow of heat from the atmosphere into the deep Atlantic and Southern Oceans due to accelerated warm saltwater subduction. The rate of this process is cyclical with periodic warming and cooling cycles over approximately 30 years. The last 30 years of the 20th century are thought to have seen this cycle in the warming phase, while the last 15 years have seen a shift to cooling phase.

To get a sense of the net energy balance, readers should turn to The American Physical Society, and its paper: "Changes in the Flow of Energy through the Earth's Climate System."

According to this source, net flow into the Earth's energy budget is $0.9W/m2$ (an imbalance of 0.4%) of which the vast majority goes into the oceans, and a much smaller proportion warms the air, and melts ice. This causes the ocean to expand bringing about rising sea levels – with a further contribution to rising sea levels from net melting of ice from glaciers and ice caps.

www.ingramcontent.com/pod-product-compliance
Lightning Source LLC
Chambersburg PA
CBHW072121270326
41931CB00010B/1631